5 Ingredient Wok Cookbook for Beginners:

Master The Art of Wok Cooking Techniques With 100 Simple and Practical 5-Ingredient Recipes You Can Prepare at The Comfort of Your Home

Michelle Tan

© **Copyright Michelle Tan 2023 - All rights reserved.**

The content contained within this book may not be reproduced, duplicated or transmitted without direct written permission from the author or the publisher.

Under no circumstances will any blame or legal responsibility be held against the publisher, or author, for any damages, reparation, or monetary loss due to the information contained within this book. Either directly or indirectly. You are responsible for your own choices, actions, and results.

Legal Notice:

This book is copyright protected. This book is only for personal use. You cannot amend, distribute, sell, use, quote or paraphrase any part, or the content within this book, without the consent of the author or publisher.

Disclaimer Notice:

Please note the information contained within this document is for educational and entertainment purposes only. All effort has been executed to present accurate, up to date, and reliable, complete information. No warranties of any kind are declared or implied. Readers acknowledge that the author is not engaging in the rendering of legal, financial, medical or professional advice. The content within this book has been derived from various sources. Please consult a licensed professional before attempting any techniques outlined in this book.

By reading this document, the reader agrees that under no circumstances is the author responsible for any losses, direct or indirect, which are incurred as a result of the use of the information contained within this document, including, but not limited to, — errors, omissions, or inaccuracies.

Table of Contents

Introduction vi

Chapter 1: Understanding the Wok! 9

    What is a Wok? 9
    History of Wok 9
    Types of Woks 11
    Benefits of a wok 13
    Uses of Wok 15
    How to Season Your Wok 18
    Choosing the Best Wok 19
    Essential Tools to Use with a Wok 20
    Types of Oils Is Used in a Wok 21
    How to Clean Your Wok 22
    Best Seasoning for Wok 24
    Troubleshooting Common Wok Issues (Q&A) 26
    Tips for Using the Wok 27
    Wok vs. Frying Pan 30

Chapter 2: Fish and Seafood Recipes 32

    1. Stir-Fried Prawns 32
    2. Shrimp Balls 34
    3. Flavorful Steamed Fish 36
    4. Stir-Fried Mussels in Black Bean Sauce 38
    5. Stir-Fried Seafood and Onions 40
    6. Wok-Fried Octopus 42
    7. Stir-Fried Cod 44
    8. Steamed Halibut in Vegetable Stock 46
    9. Scrambled Sea Bass with Scallions 48
    10. Teriyaki Salmon Fillets 50
    11. Wok-made Fish Curry 52
    12. Stir-Fried Velveted Scallops recipe 54
    13. Drunken Shrimp 56
    14. Steamed Garlic, and Scallion Salmon 58
    15. Wok-Fried Belt Fish 60
    16. Shrimp, Corn and Leeks Stir Fry 62
    17. Buttered Scallops 64
    18. Shanghainese-Style Stir-Fried Shrimp 66
    19. Wok-Fried Fish with Ginger and Scallions 68
    20. Wok-Fried Teriyaki Prawns 70
    21. Balinese Squid 72

Chapter 3: Chicken and Poultry Recipes 74

    22. Chicken Dice Lettuce Wraps 74
    23. Kung Pao Chicken 76

- 24. Scrambled Chicken with Hoisin Sauce 78
- 25. Braised Duck in Soy Sauce 80
- 26. Turkey Asparagus Stir-Fry 82
- 27. Glazed Chicken Thighs 84
- 28. Chicken with Onion and Pineapple 86
- 29. Fiery Pepper Chicken 88
- 30. Zucchini Chicken 90
- 31. Homemade Sweet and Sour Chicken 92
- 32. Chicken and Vegetables 94
- 33. Peanut Chicken Stir-Fry 96
- 34. Braised Chicken Wings 98

Chapter 4: Rice Recipes 100

- 35. Chinese Wok Fried Rice 100
- 36. Coconut Rice with Prawns 102
- 37. Rice and Grapes Stir Fry 104
- 38. Makato's Bacon Fried Rice 106
- 39. Jasmine Rice with Bok Choy 108
- 40. Corned Beef Fried Rice with Mint 110
- 41. Rice with Bacon 112
- 42. Pork Fried Rice 114
- 43. Fried Rice with Lychee 116
- 44. Wok-Fried Brown Rice 118
- 45. Apple Fried Rice 120
- 46. Asian Shrimp Rice Bowl 122
- 47. Rice fried with chicken 124
- 48. Fried rice with duck 126
- 49. Garlic Fried Rice 128

Chapter 5: Noodles Recipes 130

- 50. Garlic Noodles 130
- 51. Wok Buttered Peanut Noodles 132
- 52. Glass Noodles with Green Beans and Napa Cabbage 134
- 53. Gravy with Shrimp and Rice Noodles 136
- 54. Hakka Noodles 138
- 55. Satay Veggie Noodles 140
- 56. Broccoli and Beef Noodles 142
- 57. Dan Dan Noodles 144
- 58. Coriander with Pork Noodles 146
- 59. Chinese Birthday Noodles 148
- 60. Saucy Thai Beef Noodles 150
- 61. Chicken Stir Fry Noodles 152
- 62. Long Life Noodles 154
- 63. Sesame with Soy Sauce Noodles 156
- 64. Sirloin Stir-Fry with Ramen Noodles 158
- 65. Cilantro with Scallions Noodles 160

Chapter 6: Beef, Pork and Lamb Recipes 162

66. Gingered Beef with Broccoli 162
67. Lamb with Gingered Scallions 164
68. Pork with Mushrooms 166
69. Sichuan Pork with Peanuts 168
70. Cardamom Beef Rendang Wok 170
71. Adobo Lamb with Cabbage 172
72. Sweet-and-Sour Beef Wok Stir-Fry 174
73. Gingered Lamb with Green Beans 176
74. Beef and Zucchini Stir-Fry 178
75. Ginger Meat 180
76. Asian Pork Linguine 182
77. Celery with Beef Liver Stir Fry 184
78. Ginger and Sesame Pineapple Pork 186
79. Pepper Meat 188
80. Garlic with Braised Duck Legs 190
81. Sesame Beef 192
82. Asparagus with Steak Stir-Fry 194
83. Peppered Pork Meatballs 196

Chapter 7: Quick Recipes 198

84. Coconut Prawns on Lime Noodles 198
85. Sausage and Cabbage Wok 200
86. Bok Choy Stir-Fry 202
87. Amaranth with Vegetables 204
88. Spinach with Crispy Noodles 206
89. Butternut Squash and Bean Salad 208
90. Spiced Cashews with Fried Rice 210
91. Wok Scrambled Snow Peas 212
92. Cauliflower Curry 214
93. Rump Steak with Stir-Fried Vegetables 216
94. Tempeh with Mango and Shallots 218
95. Wok Garlic Almond Bean Stir-Fry 220
96. Spicy Red Pepper and Cucumber 222
97. Sichuan Eggplant in Sauce 224
98. Scrambled Potato and Green Beans 226
99. Bacon-Wrapped Hot Dogs 228
100. Crispy French Fries 230

Conclusion 232

Measurement Conversions 235

Introduction

Do you want to learn how to cook with a wok? Wok cooking is a tried-and-true way of preparing traditional dishes, such as stir-fry and fried recipes. It is an approach that is both easy to learn and rewarding, as the results are fast, tasty, and healthy.

Wok cooking is a traditional and versatile method of cooking that has been used in Asian cuisine for centuries. It is a simple yet efficient way of cooking that can be used to prepare a wide variety of dishes, from stir-fries to steamed dishes and soups. The key to successful wok cooking is to have the right tools, ingredients, and techniques.

This Wok Cookbook for Beginners is designed to help you learn the basics of wok cooking and to inspire you to create delicious and healthy meals for your family and friends. We will take you through the essential tools and ingredients you need, as well as the techniques and tips to make your wok cooking experience enjoyable and successful.

The first thing you need to know when learning to cook with a wok is the type of wok you should use. Traditional woks are made of carbon steel, which is lightweight and heats quickly. They are also easy to season and maintain. However, in recent years, non-stick woks have become popular due to their ease of cleaning and non-stick surface. Both types of woks are suitable for wok cooking, but it is important to choose the one that best suits your needs.

Once you have chosen your wok, it is time to learn about the ingredients. Wok cooking is all about using fresh and seasonal ingredients that can be easily found at your local grocery store. You will learn about the different meals such as meat, seafood, vegetables, and rice that can be used in wok cooking, as well as the different cooking methods to bring out the best flavors.

The techniques used in wok cooking are simple and easy to learn. The most important technique is the "stir-fry" method, where ingredients are quickly cooked over high heat with constant stirring. This technique helps to seal in the flavors and to retain the texture of the ingredients. You will also learn about other techniques such as steaming, deep-frying, and braising that can be used in wok cooking.

Throughout this cookbook, you will find a variety of recipes that are easy to follow and perfect for beginners. From classic Chinese dishes like Kung Pao Chicken and Sesame Beef, to Thai and Korean dishes like Pad Thai and Bulgogi, this cookbook has something for everyone. We also include a section on vegetarian and vegan options, as well as tips on how to make these dishes gluten-free or low-carb.

One of the best things about wok cooking is its versatility. With a wok and a few basic ingredients, you can create a wide variety of dishes from different cuisines. This cookbook includes recipes from all over Asia, including Chinese, Thai, Korean, and more. This means you can explore different flavors and techniques without ever having to leave your kitchen.

Another great aspect of wok cooking is its convenience. Wok cooking is a quick and efficient method of cooking, making it perfect for busy weeknight meals. Many of the recipes in this cookbook can be prepared in 30 minutes or less, so you can have a tasty and healthy meal on the table in no time. And with the ability to cook a variety of ingredients at once, you can save time and energy on clean-up as well.

Whether you are a beginner cook or a seasoned pro, this Wok Cookbook for Beginners is a valuable resource to help you master the art of wok cooking. With its simple and delicious recipes, helpful tips and techniques, and beautiful photography, this cookbook will inspire you to create delicious and healthy meals in the comfort of your own home. So, grab your wok, gather your ingredients, and let's start cooking!

Chapter 1:

Understanding the Wok!

What is a Wok?

A wok is a type of round-bottomed cooking pan, originating from China. It is traditionally made of carbon steel and is used for stir-frying, deep-frying, searing, and boiling, among other methods of cooking. The shape of the wok allows for even heating and easy tossing of ingredients which makes it perfect for high-heat methods of cooking such as stir-frying.

Woks are also often used in Asian cuisine to create a flavorful, savory dish by quickly cooking meats, vegetables, and other ingredients in a small amount of oil. The round bottom of the wok allows for easy movement and tossing of ingredients, while the sloping sides help to keep food from spilling out.

A wok can be used on a stovetop, or over an open flame such as a gas burner or campfire. It is also a common kitchen tool in South East Asian, Korean and Japanese cuisine. It can be also used for steaming, braising, smoking and many others as you will learn in this book.

History of Wok

The history of wok can be traced back to ancient China, where it was first used for cooking over an open flame. The wok's unique shape, which is curved at the bottom and straight at the sides, allows for efficient heat distribution and makes it ideal for stir-frying, deep-frying, boiling, steaming, and more.

The wok has been used in China for over 2,000 years, and it is believed to have originated in the Han Dynasty (206 BC - 220 AD). In ancient China, woks were made of bronze or iron, and they were used for cooking over open flames. The wok's shape was designed to maximize heat efficiency and to make it easy to toss and stir food while cooking.

During the Ming Dynasty (1368-1644), the wok became more popular and widespread. The wok's design was improved, and it started to be made of cast iron. Cast iron woks are more durable than bronze woks and they are also better at retaining heat. Cast iron woks are still very popular in China today and they are considered the best woks for stir-frying.

The wok also played an important role in the development of Cantonese cuisine, which is known for its delicate flavors and light seasoning. Cantonese cooks began using the wok for stir-frying, which involves cooking small food pieces quickly on high heat. This method preserves the natural flavors of the ingredients and creates a crispy texture.

In the 20th century, the wok became popular in other parts of Asia and around the world. This is partly attributed to the large number of Chinese immigrants who brought their culture and cuisine with them. Today, the wok can be found in kitchens all over the world, and it is used for a wide variety of dishes, from traditional Chinese dishes to Western-style stir-fries.

The wok has undergone many changes over the centuries, but the basic design has remained the same. It is still made of various materials like cast iron, carbon steel, aluminum and stainless steel. Woks made of carbon steel and cast iron are the best for stir-frying, as they can withstand high heat and they retain heat well. Aluminum and stainless-steel woks are lightweight and easy to clean.

In modern times, the wok has become a kitchen staple not only in China but all around the world. It is not only used in Chinese cuisine but also in many other Asian and Western cuisines. The wok's versatility and efficiency have made it an important tool for any home cook or professional chef who wants to create delicious, healthy meals quickly and easily.

In summary, the wok is an ancient piece of cookware that has played an important role in Chinese cuisine for over 2,000 years. Its unique shape and efficient heat distribution make it an ideal tool for a wide variety of cooking methods, from stir-frying to deep-frying and boiling. Today, the wok can be found in kitchens all over the world, and it continues to be an essential tool for creating delicious, healthy meals.

Types of Woks

There are several types of woks available on the market, each with its own unique characteristics and best uses. The most common types of woks include:

1. **Carbon Steel Woks:** Carbon steel woks are made from a thin gauge of carbon steel, which makes them lightweight and easy to handle. They heat up quickly and evenly, but they need to be seasoned before use. Carbon steel woks are great for high-heat cooking techniques such as stir-frying and deep-frying. They are also affordable and easy to find.
2. **Cast Iron Woks:** Cast iron woks are heavy and durable, but they take longer to heat up than carbon steel woks. They also retain heat well, which makes them ideal for low and slow cooking methods such as braising and stewing. Cast iron woks are also great for outdoor cooking, as they can be placed

- **Energy Efficient:** Woks are designed to be used over high heat, which means that they heat up quickly and cook food faster than other types of cookware. This makes them energy efficient and can save time and money on cooking expenses.
- **Large Cooking Surface:** Woks have a large, round cooking surface that allows for a large amount of food to be cooked at one time. This makes them ideal for large families or for cooking for a crowd.
- **Versatile Cooking Methods:** Woks can be used for different cooking methods, including steaming, deep-frying, stir-frying, and even braising. This versatility makes them a great tool for any kitchen.
- **Easy to Clean:** Woks are made of materials that are easy to clean, such as carbon steel or cast iron. These materials can withstand high heat and are easy to season, which makes them resistant to rust and corrosion.
- **Perfect for Asian Cuisine:** Woks are commonly used in Asian cuisine, specifically in Chinese, Vietnamese, and Thai dishes. They are perfect for stir-frying noodles, vegetables, and meat dishes, and for making soups and stews.
- **Enhances the flavor:** Wok cooking is a method that allows the flavors of different ingredients to blend together, creating a unique and delicious taste. The high heat and fast cooking time helps to seal in the flavors and aromas of the food, making it more delicious.
- **Healthier Cooking:** Wok cooking allows for very little oil to be used, which makes it a healthier option for cooking. This is because the food is cooked quickly over high heat, which allows it to retain more of its natural moisture and nutrients.
- **More control over heat:** Wok cooking allows the cook to have more control over the heat, which is essential for getting the perfect result. The high heat and fast cooking time allows the cook to quickly adjust the heat to achieve the desired result.

- **Can be used with different heat sources:** Woks can be used with different heat sources, including gas, electric, and induction cooktops. This makes them versatile and easy to use in any kitchen.
- **Cost-Effective:** To acquire frying pans, you'd think you'd need a lot of loans; however, the pricing of woks on the internet will astound you. To get better outcomes, you should use high-quality woks. Take into consideration that several excellent high-quality woks are reasonably priced. There is a wide range of first-rate models available to suit any budget. The cost of an electric one is higher. They're also far more expensive than standard frying pans.

Uses of Wok

The wok is a cooking tool that is used for a variety of different techniques and dishes. Some of the most common uses of a wok include:

- **Stir-frying:** This is the most common use of a wok, and it involves cooking small pieces of food quickly over high heat, while constantly stirring and tossing the ingredients. This allows the food to cook evenly and retain its natural flavors and textures.

    Did you know that there's more than one way to stir-fry? There are, in fact, four major techniques:

    Dry stir-fry. Dry stir-frying means stir-frying without the use of liquid other than a small amount of oil, and sometimes a bit of soy sauce or Shaoxing rice wine. Essentially, there is no sauce.

Wet stir-fry. Wet stir-frying is the opposite of dry stir-frying—wet stir-fries use liquid, usually rice wine, stock, or a sauce of some kind.

Clear stir-fry. Clear stir-frying allows a single ingredient to be the star of the show. Oil, salt, and a hot wok are the only items needed to bring out the best in a seasonal vegetable or a protein.

Velveting. Velveting is coating an ingredient (usually a delicate protein such as fish, shellfish, or chicken) in egg white and corn-starch before stir-frying it or before poaching it or briefly oil frying it prior to combining it with other ingredients for serving. Foods that have been velveted turn out tender and juicy.

- **Deep-frying:** This is a cooking technique that involves submerging your food in hot oil. This method cooks food quickly and ensures that all the sides are cooked simultaneously. Most foods need a coating when deep frying; therefore, you can add that batter coating you like for protection. To avoid excessively greasy foods, prepare your food properly before emersion and fry it at the right temperature. The temperature depends on the type and thickness of the food. You can use a deep-fry thermometer to keep track of the temperature. It is also important you note that you should not fill the oil more than halfway when using a wok to deep fry. Caution before anything else.
- **Searing:** A wok can be used to sear meats and vegetables at high temperatures, creating a caramelized crust on the outside while keeping the inside moist and tender.
- **Poaching:** This is a technique where food is heated while submerged in a liquid. Unlike simmering and boiling, poaching uses a lower temperature which is usually suitable for delicate foods. Too high a temperature will make the food fall apart

and dry out. Some foods you can poach in a wok include, but not limited to, fish, fruit, poultry, and eggs.

- **Braising:** This is a cooking technique that involves both wet and dry heat cooking methods. The food is usually cooked at high temperatures and then simmered in the wok in cooking liquid. You could use any liquid of your preference, whether wine, coconut milk, or beer. Unlike stewing, braising requires less liquid and involves cooking larger pieces of meat. How does a red braised pork belly sound?
- **Boiling:** A wok can also be used for boiling, such as in soups and broths.
- **Steaming:** A wok can be used to steam food, by placing a steaming basket or plate on top of the wok, and adding water to the bottom of the wok. Steaming is one of the oldest methods of Chinese cooking. The good thing is that if you have a wok, you can steam your food by inserting a steam rack. Fill the wok with the appropriate water level, boil the water to get the steam going and then place the plate with your food on top of the rack. The benefits of this cooking method are that it is gentle and healthy. It doesn't involve the use of any oils. How does that sound? Great! Right? You might be tempted to start preparing your steamed fish but let's keep going to the end.
- **Roasting:** Wok can be used for roasting nuts, seeds, and some vegetables.
- **Smoker:** Wok can be used as a smoker, by adding wood chips on the bottom of the wok and placing the food to be smoked on top.

The wok's unique shape and high, sloping sides make it ideal for these cooking techniques, allowing for easy tossing and turning of ingredients.

How to Season Your Wok

Seasoning a wok is the process of creating a natural, non-stick surface on the wok by heating it and applying oil. Seasoning is typically done on a new wok, but it can also be done on an older wok that has lost its non-stick surface. Here's how to season a wok:

- Clean the wok: Start by cleaning the wok thoroughly with warm, soapy water. Use a stiff-bristled brush or steel wool to remove any rust or discoloration. Rinse the wok well and completely dry it.
- Heat the wok: Place the wok on the stovetop over medium-high heat. Heat the wok until it is hot to the touch. This will help to open the pores of the metal and prepare it for seasoning.
- Apply oil: Use a high-heat oil such as grapeseed oil, canola oil, or vegetable oil. Place a small amount of oil in the wok and use a wok brush or a paper towel to spread the oil evenly over the surface of the wok.
- Heat the oil: Turn the heat up to high and let the oil heat for about one minute. As the oil heats, use a paper towel or a wok brush to spread the oil around the wok, making sure to coat the entire surface.
- Remove excess oil: Turn off the heat and let the wok cool down for a few minutes. Use a wok brush or a paper towel to remove any excess oil.
- Repeat: Repeat the process of heating, oiling and wiping the wok for 2-3 times.
- Store: Once your wok is seasoned, store it in a dry place and avoid washing it with soap.

It's important to note that the wok should be seasoned before the first use, and re-seasoned periodically, depending on the usage, especially if it starts to rust or lose its non-stick surface.

By seasoning a wok, you will create a natural, non-stick surface that will make cooking with your wok much easier. The seasoning will also help to protect the wok from rust and discoloration, and it will give the wok a unique patina that will improve with use over time.

Choosing the Best Wok

Selecting the best wok for you will depend on your personal preferences and needs. Here are some few things to consider when you want to choose a wok:

- **Material:** Woks can be made of carbon steel, cast iron, aluminum, or stainless steel. Carbon steel woks are lightweight and heat quickly, but require seasoning before use. Cast iron woks are heavy and retain heat well, but take longer to heat up. Aluminum woks are lightweight and heat quickly, but can be prone to warping. Stainless steel woks are durable and easy to clean, but do not heat as evenly as other materials.
- **Size:** Woks are available in a range of sizes, from small to large. Consider the number of people you will be cooking for, as well as the size of your stovetop and storage space.
- **Shape:** Woks can have round or flat bottoms. Round-bottomed woks are traditional and are best for use on gas stoves, while flat-bottomed woks are more versatile and can be used on electric or gas stoves.
- **Handle:** Consider the type of handle that is most comfortable for you to use. Some woks have wooden handles, while others have metal handles.
- **Brand:** Look for reputable brands that are known for producing high-quality woks.

Ultimately, you should choose a wok that is made of a durable material, fits your cooking needs, and is comfortable for you to use.

Essential Tools to Use with a Wok

When cooking with a wok, there are several essential tools that can make the process easier and more efficient. Some of the most important tools to use with a wok include:

- Wok spatula: A wok spatula is a flat and wide utensil that is designed specifically for use with a wok. It has a long handle that keeps your hand away from the heat and a wide surface area that allows you to stir and toss ingredients quickly and easily.
- Wok ladle: A wok ladle is a large spoon with a long handle that is designed for use with a wok. It is used for scooping and serving soups, broths, and sauces. Wok ladles are typically made of metal and they come in different shapes and sizes.
- Wok Tongs: Wok tongs: Wok tongs are a type of tongs that are designed for use with a wok. They are used for flipping and turning ingredients, and can also be used to remove food from the wok. Wok tongs are typically made of metal and they come in different shapes and sizes.
- **Wok lid:** A wok lid is a cover that is used to trap steam and heat inside the wok. This can be used to cook food more quickly and evenly and to keep food warm after it is cooked.
- **Wok ring:** A wok ring is a metal ring that sits on top of a burner and supports the wok. It is used to steady the wok and prevent it from tipping over. It is especially useful if you have a gas stove with small burners.
- **Steaming basket:** A steaming basket is a metal basket that sits inside a wok and is used to steam food. It is typically made of bamboo or metal, and it allows the food to be cooked by the steam rising from the water in the wok.
- **Wok brush:** A wok brush is a brush with stiff bristles that is designed for use with a wok. It is used for cleaning the wok,

and also for spreading oil or sauces evenly over the surface of the wok. Wok brushes are typically made of bamboo or metal.
- **Wok thermometer:** A wok thermometer is a device used to measure the temperature of the oil in a wok. It is especially useful for deep-frying, as it allows you to maintain a consistent temperature and prevent the oil from becoming too hot or too cold.
- **Wok stand:** A wok stand is a metal stand that is used to hold a wok over an open flame. It is especially useful for outdoor cooking, as it allows you to cook with a wok over a campfire or grill.

When cooking with a wok, it's important to have the right tools on hand in order to make the cooking process as easy and efficient as possible. The above are all essential tools that can help you create delicious and authentic Asian dishes with your wok.

It's important to note that the wok is a multipurpose tool that can be used for a wide variety of dishes, and the tools you will need will vary depending on what you are cooking. Having a set of these essential tools on hand will give you the flexibility to cook a wide range of dishes and techniques, and will make the process more enjoyable and efficient.

Types of Oils Is Used in a Wok

There are several types of oils that are commonly used in a wok, each with their own unique characteristics and benefits. Some popular options include:

- **Vegetable oil:** This oil is a common choice for wok cooking due to its high smoke point of around 400°F. It is a blend of different types of oils and has a neutral flavor, making it a versatile oil for many dishes.

- Peanut oil: This oil has a high smoke point of around 446°F, making it a great choice for high-heat cooking like stir-frying. It also contains a mild, nutty flavor that complements many Asian dishes.
- **Canola oil:** This oil also has a high smoke point, around 400°F. It is also a good source of monounsaturated fats, which are beneficial for heart health. Additionally, it has a neutral flavor that does not overpower other ingredients.
- **Sesame oil:** This oil has a lower smoke point of around 350°F, so it is best used as a finishing oil or for low-heat cooking. Its strong, nutty flavor is often used in Asian cuisine as a flavoring.
- **Coconut oil:** This oil has a high smoke point of around 350°F and has a distinct coconut flavor. It is a popular choice for certain Asian dishes, particularly Thai and Indian cuisine.
- **Ghee:** Ghee is clarified butter, it has a smoke point of around 485°F and has a rich, buttery flavor. It is commonly used as a cooking oil in Indian cuisines.

It's important to note that the oil's smoke point is the degree (temperature) at which the oil starts to smoke and break down, which can give an unpleasant flavor to food. It's always best to choose an oil with a high smoke point for high-heat cooking like stir-frying.

When stir-frying, a combination of oil with a high smoke point and oil with a strong flavor is often used. For example, a mixture of peanut oil and sesame oil. The peanut oil can handle the high heat while the sesame oil adds flavor.

How to Clean Your Wok

Cleaning a wok can seem like a daunting task, especially if you're not sure how to do it properly. However, with the proper tools and techniques, you can easily keep your wok in top condition for years to come.

The first step in cleaning your wok is to remove any remaining food or debris. Use a metal spatula or a wooden spoon to scrape off any bits of food that may be stuck to the sides or bottom of the wok. You can also use a paper towel or damp cloth to wipe down the inside of the wok.

Next, fill the wok with warm water and a small amount of dish soap. Scrub the inside of the wok using a non-abrasive brush or sponge, being sure to pay extra attention to any areas that have food stains or build-up. Be sure to also scrub the outside of the wok, including the handle.

Once you've finished scrubbing, thoroughly rinse the wok using warm water to get rid of any remaining soap residue. If there are any hard-to-remove stains or build-up, you can try using a mixture of water and baking soda to gently scrub the area.

After rinsing, dry the wok thoroughly with a clean cloth or paper towel. It's important to dry the wok completely to prevent rust or other damage.

If your wok has a non-stick coating, be sure to use a non-abrasive sponge or brush when cleaning, and avoid using any harsh detergents or abrasive materials. Additionally, you should avoid using metal utensils on a non-stick wok, as they can scratch the coating and damage the wok.

To maintain the condition of your wok, it's important to properly store it when not in use. You should always dry the wok thoroughly before storing it, and it's best to hang it or store it in a dry place. If you're storing your wok in a cabinet or drawer, be sure to cover it with a clean cloth or paper towel to protect it from dust or other debris.

Regularly cleaning your wok is crucial to maintaining its appearance and longevity. With the right techniques and, tools you can easily keep your wok in top condition and ensure that it's always ready to use when you need it.

Best Seasoning for Wok

Cooking with a wok brings timely enjoyment and simple preparation tasks. To make the use of this special pan even more efficient and effective and to guarantee a full-bodied taste experience, seasoning is needed as it is crucial to utilize the proper seasonings in order to really bring out the flavor and scent of your foods. Here are some of the best seasonings to use when cooking with a wok:

- **Curry:** As a powder or paste, a colorful mixture of spices. There are countless varieties with different degrees of spiciness, so always use a new curry spice sparingly at first. In the case of finished pastes, the green one is fiery hot, the red one a bit and the yellow one much milder.
- **Turmeric:** Root that provides a tart taste and orange-red color. Usually dried as a powder, more and more often available as a fresh root from us. Dice or grate finely – wear disposable gloves when doing this.
- **Tamarind:** Legume of the sour date, mostly sold as a paste (Asian shops). It sours and seasons food. Alternatively, you can use 2 tablespoons each of hoisin sauce and lemon juice.
- **Soy sauce:** This is a staple in many Asian cuisines, and it's a great addition to any wok dish. It adds a rich, savory flavor that pairs well with meats, vegetables, and noodles.
- **Oyster sauce:** Oyster sauce is another Asian staple that's perfect for wok cooking. It has a sweet, salty flavor that complements meats and vegetables alike.
- Fish sauce: Fish sauce is a pungent, salty sauce made from fermented fish. It's a common ingredient in Southeast Asian cuisine and adds a unique, umami flavor to dishes.

- **Sesame oil:** Sesame oil is a fragrant oil that's often used as a finishing oil in wok dishes. It's great for adding a nutty, toasted flavor to your food.
- **Hoisin sauce:** Hoisin sauce is a sweet, savory sauce that's commonly used in Chinese cuisine. It's perfect for adding a touch of sweetness to meats and vegetables.
- **Rice vinegar:** Rice vinegar is a mild, slightly sweet vinegar that's a great addition to wok dishes. It adds a tangy, acidic flavor that helps to balance out the rich, savory flavors of your ingredients.
- **Garlic and ginger:** Garlic and ginger are two essential seasonings that are commonly used in wok dishes. They add a pungent, aromatic flavor that pairs well with a wide variety of ingredients.
- **Chili flakes or paste:** Chili flakes or paste are an amazing way to add a bit of heat to your wok dishes. They're perfect for creating spicy, flavorful dishes that will wake up your taste buds.
- **Chinese five-spice powder:** Chinese five-spice powder is a blend of spices that's commonly used in Chinese cuisine. It typically includes cinnamon, star anise, fennel seed, cloves, and Szechuan pepper. It gives a warm, aromatic and flavorful taste to the dishes.
- **Coriander:** Coriander is a herb that's commonly used in Asian cuisine. It has a fresh, citrusy flavor that's perfect for adding a touch of freshness to your wok dishes.

When seasoning your wok dishes, it's important to remember that less is often more. Start with small amounts of seasonings and then add more to taste. This will help you to achieve the perfect balance of flavors without overpowering your ingredients.

Troubleshooting Common Wok Issues (Q&A)

Q: My wok is not properly seasoned. How can I fix this?

A: To properly season a wok, heat the wok on high heat till it starts to smoke. Then, using a paper towel or cloth, coat the wok with a small amount of oil (vegetable or peanut oil work well). Continue to heat the wok, using a metal spatula to scrape the surface and distribute the oil evenly. Once the wok has cooled, repeat this process several times until the surface of the wok becomes dark and glossy.

Q: My wok is rusting, what should I do?

A: If your wok is rusting, it means that it's not being properly dried and stored. To prevent rust, be sure to dry your wok thoroughly after each use and store it in a dry place. You also can try to use a rust remover solution to remove the rust and then apply a coat of oil to the wok to protect it from rusting again.

Q: My wok has scratches on the surface, what should I do?

A: If your wok has scratches on the surface, it's likely that you've been using metal utensils or abrasive materials when cleaning it. To prevent scratches, use non-abrasive tools and materials when cleaning your wok, and avoid using metal utensils. If the scratches are deep, it may be time to replace the wok.

Q: My wok has a sticky surface, what should I do?

A: If your wok has a sticky surface, it's likely that food residue or oil has built up on the surface. To remove the stickiness, you can try scrubbing the wok with a mixture of baking soda and water, or using a specialized wok cleaner. Be sure to rinse the wok thoroughly and dry it completely before using it again.

Q: My wok has warped, what should I do?

A: Warping can be caused by subjecting the wok to sudden temperature changes (such as running cold water over a hot wok) or by uneven heating. To fix a warped wok, you can try to reshape it by heating it over high heat and then using a metal spatula or tongs to press and shape the wok back into its original form. However, if the warping is severe, the wok may need to be replaced.

Q: My wok has a non-stick coating that is peeling, what should I do?

A: If your wok has a non-stick coating that is peeling, it's likely that you've been using metal utensils or abrasive materials when cleaning it, or exposing it to high heat. To prevent peeling, use non-abrasive tools and materials when cleaning your wok, and avoid using metal utensils and exposing it to high heat. If the coating is severely damaged, it may be time to replace the wok.

Q: My wok is not properly seasoned. How can I fix this?

A: To properly season a wok, heat the wok on high heat until it starts to smoke. Then, using a paper towel or cloth, coat the wok with a small amount of oil (vegetable or peanut oil work well). Continue to heat the wok, using a metal spatula to scrape the surface and distribute the oil evenly. Once the wok has cooled, repeat this process several times until the surface of the wok becomes dark and glossy.

Tips for Using the Wok

Cooking with a wok is an art, and there are a some tips and tricks you can use to make cooking easier. We've listed some of these helpful tips below for any beginner who wants to start cooking with their wok:

Clean the Wok's surface before you begin cooking.

When cooking in a wok, it's a good idea to season the surface first. As a result, your food will not cling to the surface. For example, if you're cooking chicken and it sticks to the pan, it'll burn before it's finished. As a result, not only will the meal's flavor change, but it will also be difficult to transfer the remaining food about the wok. As a result, make your wok non-stick by pouring oil into it before cooking and draining it into a heat-resistant container once it reaches smoking temperatures. After that, add some more cooking oil to make it easier to turn and toss the meal around.

Cooking isn't limited to stir-frying.

Because it can be used for more than simply stir-frying, the wok is extremely cost-effective. Because it uses significantly less oil than a frying pan, it is great for deep frying. It can also be used to make stews, boil water, and smoke meals. Others use it to steam food, such as by inserting a bamboo steamer into the wok. Steaming can also be accomplished by placing metal trivets in the bottom of a wok, then placing a dish on top of the trivet and covering it. All of this is possible with a wok, and you may enjoy a wide range of exquisite cuisine once you learn how to make them.

Season every time you cook

When stir-frying, the most frustrating thing that can happen is that your chicken sticks, and then you scrape it off and have something adhere to the wok that will burn prior to the dish finishing. It alters the flavor and makes moving meals challenging. To prevent that, add some oil, swirl it over the wok's cooking surface, and allow the oil to become blazing hot. After that, transfer it into a heat-resistant container and add new oil to cook with. That is how a wok can be converted into a non-stick pan.

Choose the Best Wok for You

Although a good wok is essential in a family, it is best to select the suitable wok based on the type of stove you have at home. When utilizing an electric burner, for example, the type of wok you use is different than when using a gas flame stove. You can also select them according to the type of ingredient they contain. Many people like Chinese carbon steel woks because they heat and cool quickly. Consider the handles. Depending on your demands, you may like one long handle or two ear handles. Woks, on the other hand, are quite sturdy and safe, and one with a diameter of at least 12 inches is perfect for usage at home.

Divide the Recipes

When you have recipes that require different cooking speeds, you must prepare them separately. Assume you have some meat and some crunchy vegetables, for example. Rather than cooking them all at once, consider including the vegetables near the end to get the best of both worlds. After that, add the meat and serve, as both have been properly cooked. Because of the changed timing, you won't have to worry about one being overcooked and the other being raw. Also, if you want to create extra meals, avoid repeating the recipes. It's best to repeat a process than stir-fry a large amount of food because not all of it will be scorched. Optionally, if you're cooking for a large gathering, avoid making everything a stir fry because it's time-consuming. Prepare a stew, divide the rice, and get some cold dishes ready.

Recognize the Appropriate Temperature

Assume you want to make a typical stir-fry but don't have a wok. It is best to do it on a very high heat setting. As a result, depending on the dish, increase the heat to attain the best outcomes. When making a stir fry, a little smoke or hissing isn't as bad. Make sure your oil isn't too hot before adding your seasonings. As a result, season the wok to keep the aromatics from adhering to it rather than blending with your food. If you like chives, garlic, and other flavors, add the oil after seasoning to extract their flavor without burning when the heat is increased.

Taking Care of Your Work Is Simple

In Chinese households, the wok is a common item of cookware. As a result, they understand how to care for it appropriately. Assume this is your first time using it. To begin with, they are indestructible, so you may thoroughly clean them if necessary. However, don't forget to season it after it's clean. A scoop is superior than most instruments for removing stock water and oil as part of wok maintenance because it won't chip the wok's surface. The bamboo brush can also be used to clean plates while the food is still warm. Check that all bristles are of good quality and will not melt. When using a wok, a slotted spoon or ladles are also useful.

Wok vs. Frying Pan

A wok and a frying pan are both types of pans that are used for cooking, but they have some key differences.

A wok is a round-bottomed pan that is typically used in Chinese and other Asian cuisines. It is made of carbon steel or cast iron and has high, sloping sides, which makes it ideal for stir-frying, deep-frying, boiling, steaming, and braising. The round bottom and high sides of the wok allow for even heat distribution and efficient stirring and tossing of ingredients.

A frying pan is, on the other hand, a flat-bottomed pan that has lower, sloping sides. It is typically used for pan-frying, sautéing, and browning. Frying pans come in various materials like stainless steel, aluminium and non-stick. The flat bottom of the frying pan allows for even heat distribution and easy flipping of ingredients, but it is not as good for stir-frying or deep-frying as a wok.

In summary, a wok is better for high-heat cooking methods like stir-frying, deep-frying, and boiling, while a frying pan is better for pan-frying, sautéing, and browning. Both pans have their own unique features and uses, so it really depends on the type of cooking you plan to do.

Chapter 2:

Fish and Seafood Recipes

1. Stir-Fried Prawns

If you're looking for a quick, easy, and delicious dish to whip up on a weeknight, this recipe is perfect. It's fast, filling, and full of fresh ingredients with tons of flavor. Plus, you can enjoy it without feeling guilty. This dish is not only healthy, but also low-carb!

Prep Time: 10 minutes
Cook Time: 5 minutes
Servings: 2

Ingredients:

- 1 lb. large prawns, peeled and deveined
- 2 cloves garlic, minced
- 1 red bell pepper, sliced
- 2 tablespoons vegetable oil
- 2 tablespoons soy sauce

Instructions:

1. Heat a wok over high heat.
2. Add the oil and when it's hot, add the garlic and stir-fry for about half a minute.
3. Add the prawns and bell pepper and stir-fry for 4 minutes or until the prawns are pink and cooked through.
4. Add in the soy sauce, and cook as you stir for a minute until the prawns are well coated.
5. Serve immediately, garnished with cilantro, green onion if desired.

Nutritional information per serving:

Calories: 224 Fats: 9g Carbs: 8.2g Proteins: 28.1g

2. Shrimp Balls

This recipe is for a simple and delicious shrimp ball dish that is perfect for a quick meal. This recipe for shrimp balls is a fantastic way to get your children excited about eating their vegetables as well as a healthy alternative to traditional fried appetizers like mozzarella sticks.

Prep Time: 10 minutes
Cook Time: 4 minutes
Servings: 35 Shrimp Balls

Ingredients:

- 1 pound medium shrimp, shelled and deveined
- 8 water chestnuts, finely chopped
- 1 green onion, finely chopped
- 2 teaspoons soy sauce
- ¼ teaspoon sesame oil

Instructions:

1. Soak your shrimp in some salted water for at least 5 minutes. Then rinse them with some cold water and pat dry with some paper towels.
2. Process both your shrimp and your chestnuts together in a blender. Using a medium to a large-sized mixing bowl, mix all of your ingredients until they begin to form a fine mixture.
3. Using your hand, roll your mixture between your hands to form small balls.
4. Once your balls are made, heat a generous amount of oil in a large-sized wok over high heat. Carefully and slowly add your shrimp balls to the wok, making sure not to overcrowd the wok.
5. Fry up your shrimp balls for at least 3 to 4 minutes or until they are crisp and golden in colour.
6. Remove the balls from the oil and place them onto a plate to drain the excess oil using a paper towel.
7. Serve the shrimp balls while they are still hot and enjoy!

Nutritional information per serving:

Calories: 21 Fats: 0.3g Carbs: 1.4g Proteins: 3.1g

3. Flavorful Steamed Fish

Fish is a basic part of most people's diet, but it's hard to find the perfect fish recipe. What's right for your taste buds may not be good for the environment. Are you trying to avoid mercury and other pollutants? Tired of cleaning up a mess when you cook wild salmon? Steam fish with these simple tips to get the best flavors and avoid these mistakes.

Prep Time: 5 minutes
Cook Time: 12 minutes
Servings: 4

Ingredients:

- 1½ tablespoons light soy sauce
- 2 scallions, cut lengthwise
- 2 tablespoons vegetable oil
- 10-ounce fillet of white fish
- ¼ teaspoon salt

Instructions:

1. Bring to boil 1/8 cup of water and combine the salt, light soy sauce, and hot water in a small bowl.
2. Prepare a steamer.
3. Rinse your fish fillet and place it on a heat-resistant platter that will fit in the steamer. Place it carefully in the steamer and set the heat to medium.
4. Steam for 10 minutes, covered, until done.
5. Remove from the steamer and carefully drain any liquid that has accumulated on the plate.
6. Top the steamed fish with the onions.
7. Add the vegetable oil in a wok and heat over medium-high heat to create the sauce.
8. Fry for 1 minute and cook for 30 seconds after adding the white sections of the scallions.
9. Toss in the soy sauce mixture.
10. Cook for about 30 seconds after bringing the mixture to a boil.
11. Immediately pour this mixture over the fish and serve!

Nutritional information per serving:

Calories: 239 Fats: 17g Carbs: 3g Proteins: 19g

4. Stir-Fried Mussels in Black Bean Sauce

There are still a few months of cold weather ahead, and the thought of another winter dish doesn't always sound too appealing. So why shouldn't you switch things up a bit? This is perfect for days where you want something cozy, but don't want to go too heavy on the carbs or salt. Stir-fried mussels in black bean sauce will change your life for all eternity.

Prep Time: 10 minutes
Cook Time: 7 minutes
Servings: 4

Ingredients:

- 1 lb. mussels
- 3 cloves of garlic, minced
- 1 tbsp. black bean sauce
- 1 tbsp. soy sauce

- 1 tbsp. vegetable oil

Instructions:

1. In a large bowl, thoroughly rinse the mussels under running water to get rid of any debris or dirt. Discard any mussels that are open and do not close when tapped.
2. Heat a wok over high heat. Once hot, add the vegetable oil.
3. Add the minced garlic and stir-fry until fragrant or for 30 seconds.
4. Add the mussels to the wok and stir-fry for 2-3 minutes or until they start to open.
5. Add the black bean sauce and soy sauce and stir to coat the mussels evenly. Continue to stir-fry for 2-3 more minutes or until the mussels are fully cooked and heated through.
6. Serve the Wok-Stir-Fried Mussels in Black Bean Sauce immediately with steamed rice or a side of vegetables. Enjoy!

Nutritional information per serving:

Calories: 485 Fats: 35.7g Carbs: 17.6g Proteins: 28.6g

5. Stir-Fried Seafood and Onions

For some people, cooking stir-fried seafood and onions is a way of life. To others, it might seem like a strange idea and they would rather stick to something they already know - like pizza or barbecue. However, those who run their own kitchens realize the value of cooking a good stir-fry because it is fast and easy. Because it is so simple to make, you can add one new dish to your repertoire and you will be very pleased with the results.

Prep Time: 5 minutes
Cook Time: 9 minutes
Servings: 2

Ingredients:

- 1 tablespoon cooking oil

- 9 ounces frozen mixed seafood, thawed and defrosted
- 1 tablespoon soy sauce
- Salt, to taste
- 5 stalks spring onions, sliced

Instructions:

1. Heat the cooking oil on high heat in a wok and add the garlic. Cook for 2 minutes or until aromatic.
2. After that, add the seafood and stir-fry for about 5 minutes.
3. Add soy sauce to taste. Cook for roughly 2 minutes in a stir-fry pan. If it still needs flavor, season with salt to taste.
4. Toss in the cut spring onions and cook until they start to wilt. Serve right away.

Nutritional information per serving:

Calories: 221 Fats: 8.5g Carbs: 13g Proteins: 20g

6. Wok-Fried Octopus

Eating octopus might not seem like the most appetizing experience, but if you think about it, octopus tastes amazing! Octopuses are versatile and can either be boiled in a delicious garlic sauce or fried like this recipe. Truthfully, cooking octopus can be intimidating. After all, it's a rather ugly creature. And while peeling it isn't exactly easy, the finished product is definitely worth the effort! Of course, you can choose to eat your octopus any way you like.

Prep Time: 8 minutes
Cook Time: 5 minutes
Servings: 4

Ingredients:

- 1 lb. octopus, cleaned and cut into bite-sized pieces
- 2 tbsp. vegetable oil
- 2 cloves of garlic, minced

- 1 tsp. soy sauce
- 1 tsp. sesame oil

Instructions:

1. Heat a wok over high heat. Add the oil and tilt the pan to coat the bottom evenly.
2. Add the garlic and stir-fry until fragrant or for about 30 seconds.
3. Add the octopus and stir-fry for 2-3 minutes, until the octopus is cooked through and slightly charred.
4. Add sesame oil and the soy sauce, and continue stir-frying for another minute.
5. Serve immediately with steamed rice, if desired.

Nutritional information per serving:

Calories: 664 Fats: 27.1g Carbs: 42.1g Proteins: 64.2g

Note: Precooking the octopus, either by boiling or sous-vide is preferred to ensure the perfect texture, which you may increase or decrease the stir-frying time. Also, if you want it spicy, you can add some chili flakes or chili paste to taste.

7. Stir-Fried Cod

If you're looking for an easy, tasty, and healthy recipe to cook up, then congratulations: You've found it. This recipe takes less than 20 minutes to whip up and is not only budget-friendly but also a breeze to clean up. Give it a shot! I'm so excited to share this awesome stir-fried cod recipe with you all today.

Prep Time: 10 minutes
Cook Time: 8 minutes
Servings: 2

Ingredients:

- 1 lb. cod fillet, cut into bite-sized pieces
- 1 cup sliced bell peppers (red, yellow, and green)
- ½ cup sliced onions
- 2 tbsp. soy sauce
- 2 tbsp. vegetable oil

Instructions:

1. Heat a wok over high heat. Add the vegetable oil and swirl to coat the bottom of the wok.
2. Add the sliced onions and bell peppers to the wok and stir-fry for 2-3 minutes, until the vegetables are just starting to soften.
3. Add the cod to the wok and stir-fry for 2-3 minutes, until the fish is just starting to turn opaque.
4. Add the soy sauce and continue stir-frying for 2 more minutes, until the fish is cooked through and the vegetables are tender.
5. Serve the wok-stir-fried cod immediately, garnished with fresh cilantro or green onions if desired. Enjoy!

Nutritional information per serving:

Calories: 290 Fats: 14.9g Carbs: 16.9g Proteins: 22.9g

8. Steamed Halibut in Vegetable Stock

For many people, cooking can be a truly rewarding experience. It is a shared activity that brings people together and lets them spend time with the ones they love. There's no better way to nourish your family and enjoy the time spent together than by preparing something delicious from scratch. Halibut is a popular fish used in various types of cuisine. This tasty fish has plenty of health benefits, but steamed halibut is also very easy to cook.

Prep Time: 10 minutes
Cook Time: 3 minutes
Servings: 4

Ingredients:

- 2 teaspoons fresh ginger, minced
- 4 Halibut fillets, boned and skinned
- ½ teaspoon Cayenne

- 1 cup vegetable stock
- 2 tablespoons grapeseed oil

Instructions:

1. Heat grapeseed oil in the wok on medium-high and add ginger.
2. Sauté for about 2-3 minutes. Turn the heat down to medium-low.
3. Add Halibut and vegetable stock and cook until halibut is soft.
4. Add Cayenne and cook until fragrant.
5. Serve over noodles or rice.

Nutritional information per serving:

Calories: 226 Fats: 2.8g Carbs: 24g Proteins: 25g

9. Scrambled Sea Bass with Scallions

Sea bass is a healthy, delicious and simple to prepare fish. But if you're anything like me you might find that preparing it for dinner can turn into a big mess. And who wants to spend their whole evening cleaning up? That is the reason I want to share my recipe for scrambled sea bass with scallions. The next time you are in a bind, recycle an old recipe and try this dish—it's incredibly fast and easy to make. This dish is also surprisingly healthy and cheap!

Prep Time: 10 minutes
Cook Time: 6 minutes
Servings: 3

Ingredients:

- 3 lb. sea bass, cut into bite-sized pieces

- 3 scallions, thinly sliced
- 2 tbsp. vegetable oil
- 1 tsp. soy sauce
- 1 tsp. sesame oil

Instructions:

1. Heat a wok over medium-high heat. Add the vegetable oil and allow it to heat up.
2. Add the sea bass pieces to the wok and stir-fry until they are cooked through and lightly browned or for 2-3 minutes.
3. Add the scallions and continue to stir-fry for another 1-2 minutes.
4. Add in sesame oil and the soy sauce and stir and cook for an additional minute.
5. Serve the wok-scrambled sea bass and scallions immediately, garnished with additional scallions if desired.

Nutritional information per serving:

Calories: 254 Fats: 11.6g Carbs: 1.4g Proteins: 34.1g

10. Teriyaki Salmon Fillets

Don't know how to make teriyaki salmon fillets? Want to impress your dinner guests? Teriyaki Salmon Fillets is a quick and easy dish that is perfect for any day of the week. Great for both grilling and pan frying, it pairs well with other seafood, vegetables and rice dishes.

Prep Time: 6 minutes
Cook Time: 8 minutes
Servings: 4

Ingredients:

- 4 salmon fillets
- ¼ cup soy sauce
- 2 tbsp. brown sugar
- 1 tbsp. rice vinegar
- 2 cloves minced garlic

Instructions:

1. In a medium bowl, mix together the minced garlic brown sugar, rice vinegar, and soy sauce, to create the teriyaki sauce.
2. Heat a wok over high heat.
3. Add the salmon fillets to the wok and cook until they are cooked through, or for 2-3 minutes per side.
4. Pour the teriyaki sauce over the salmon fillets and stir to coat.
5. Cook for 1-2 more minutes, or until the sauce is heated through.
6. Serve the teriyaki salmon fillets over rice or with vegetables. Enjoy!

Nutritional information per serving:

Calories: 326 Fats: 11.4g Carbs: 27.6g Proteins: 30.1g

11. Wok-made Fish Curry

The curry powder provides a rich and flavorful base, while the coconut milk adds a creamy and slightly sweet finish. The fish cooks quickly and is a perfect Proteins to pair with the curry.

Prep Time: 10 minutes
Cook Time: 10 minutes
Servings: 4

Ingredients:

- 1 lb. fish fillets (your choice of fish)
- 2 tbsp. curry powder
- 1 can coconut milk
- 1 onion, sliced
- 2 cloves garlic, minced

Instructions:

1. Place a large skillet or wok on medium-high heat.
2. Put in the garlic and onion and stir-fry for 1-2 minutes until softened.
3. Add the curry powder and stir-fry for another minute.
4. Add in the coconut milk and allow it to simmer.
5. Add the fish fillets and cook until the fish is cooked through or for about 7 minutes.
6. Serve over rice.

Nutritional information per serving:

Calories: 300 Fats: 21g Proteins: 22g Carbs: 7g

12. Stir-Fried Velveted Scallops recipe

I know what you're thinking, I can't stand the taste of ginger and those scallops look awful... but wait! Before you go on to read something else, I'm going to tell you that this recipe is actually pretty good. In fact, it's quite tasty! If you're interested in finding out more then please keep reading.

Prep Time: 5 minutes
Cook Time: 4 minutes
Servings: 4

Ingredients:

- 1 lb. scallops
- 1 tbsp. corn-starch
- 1 tsp. soy sauce
- 1 tbsp. vegetable oil
- 1 tbsp. scallions, finely chopped

Instructions:

1. In a small bowl, mix together the corn-starch and soy sauce.
2. Add the scallops to the mixture and toss to evenly coat.
3. Place a wok over high heat, add vegetable oil and eat it.
4. When the oil is heated, add the scallops to the wok and stir-fry for about 2-3 minutes, or until cooked through and lightly browned on the outside.
5. Add the scallions to the skillet and stir-fry for an additional minute.
6. Serve the stir-fried scallops hot, and enjoy!

Nutritional information per serving:

Calories: 235 Fats: 11.2g Carbs: 13.5g Proteins: 20.4g

13. Drunken Shrimp

This recipe is a Chinese dish that is easy to make and delicious, it's typically served as an appetizer or a main dish. The name "drunken" shrimp refers to the Shaoxing wine used in the marinade, which is used to give the shrimp a unique and bold flavor.

Prep Time: 8 minutes
Cook Time: 6 minutes
Servings: 3

Ingredients:

- 1 lb. large shrimp, peeled and deveined
- ¼ cup Shaoxing wine (Chinese rice wine)
- 2 cloves of garlic, minced
- 1 tbsp. soy sauce
- 1 tbsp. cornstarch

Instructions:

1. In a bowl, mix together the Shaoxing wine, soy sauce, minced garlic, and cornstarch to create a marinade. Add the shrimp and toss to coat. Marinate for at least 20 minutes.
2. Heat a wok or large skillet on medium heat. Remove the shrimp from the marinade and reserve the marinade.
3. Put the shrimp to the skillet and cook until they are pink and slightly charred or for about 2-3 minutes on each side.
4. Reduce heat to medium-low, add the reserved marinade, and stir until the sauce thickens and coats the shrimp.
5. Serve hot as a side dish or over steamed rice.

Nutritional information per serving:

Calories: 301 Fats: 7.6g Carbs: 11.2g Proteins: 23.3g

14. Steamed Garlic, and Scallion Salmon

Is there anything better than a pleasantly crunchy salmon filet? The answer is most likely no, but if you're looking for something that tastes like summer, maybe you should try steamed garlic and scallion salmon. It has a rich taste that tastes almost like it came straight out of the ocean! It's flavorful, easy-to-make quick meal perfect for these challenging times.

Prep Time: 10 minutes
Cook Time: 10 minutes
Servings: 4

Ingredients:

- 1½ pounds fresh salmon fillet
- 4 garlic cloves, crushed and chopped
- 4 scallions, minced
- ¼ cup dark soy sauce
- 1 tablespoon Shaoxing cooking wine

Instructions:

1. Cut the salmon fillet into 4 pieces and put in a pie pan or shallow dish for steaming.
2. Lightly score the fillets about halfway through with perpendicular cuts 1 inch apart.
3. In a small bowl, mix the scallions, soy sauce, and wine together to form a coarse pesto.
4. Spread the pesto on top of the fillet, being sure to press it into the cuts.
5. In the wok, bring 1 inch of water to a boil over high heat. Place a rack in the wok and the pan on the rack.
6. Cover and steam the fish for 5 minutes per inch of thickness for medium rare. It will be opaque and flaky when poked with a fork or chopstick.
7. Serve over rice.

Nutritional information per serving:

Calories: 287 Fats: 9g Carbs: 19g Proteins: 24.5g

15. Wok-Fried Belt Fish

Here's a quick and tasty recipe for your next family meal. This dish is called "wok-fried belt fish" in the Philippines, and it can be made with any type of belt fish. It's an easy-to-follow, delicious meal that both adults and children will love.

Prep Time: 15 minutes
Cook Time: 10 minutes
Servings: 4

Ingredients:

- 1 pound belt fish fillets
- 1 tablespoon oil
- 1 garlic clove, minced
- 2 green onions, sliced
- 2 tablespoons soy sauce

Instructions:

1. Heat a large skillet wok or over high heat. Add the oil and swirl over to coat every part of the pan.
2. Add the belt fish fillets to the pan and cook until they are cooked through and golden brown, for about 4 minutes on each side,.
3. Add the garlic and green onions to the pan and stir-fry for 1-2 minutes, until fragrant.
4. Pour in the soy sauce and stir to coat the fish and vegetables.
5. Serve the wok-fried belt fish immediately, with rice or noodles as a side dish. Enjoy!

Nutritional information per serving:

Calories: 207 Fats: 15g Carbs: 1g Proteins: 14g

16. Shrimp, Corn and Leeks Stir Fry

A Shrimp, Corn and Leeks Stir Fry is a delightful dish that is perfect for a hot summer day. This recipe takes barely any time to prepare, but tastes like an authentic dish you'd order out of a Chinese restaurant. The key to this recipe is to use as few dishes as possible. If everything ahead of time, then all you need is a wok or frying pan and a plate for serving.

Prep Time: 5 minutes
Cook Time: 5 minutes
Servings: 2

Ingredients:

- 1 sliced carrot
- ½ pound shrimp
- 1 cup drained corn
- 1 cup sliced onions

- 1 Tbsp. oil

Instructions:

1. Marinade shrimp in Super foods marinade.
2. Stir-fry drained shrimp in coconut oil for 2 minutes, add all vegetables and Stir-fry for 2 more minutes.
3. Add the rest of the marinade and Stir-fry for a minute. Serve with brown rice or quinoa.

Nutritional information per serving:

Calories: 239 Fats: 9g Carbs: 19g Proteins: 22g

17. Buttered Scallops

This delicious and easy wok-made Buttered Scallops recipe is perfect for a quick weeknight dinner. The scallops are cooked in butter and olive oil, which give them a rich and buttery flavor. The garlic powder adds a subtle hint of garlic, while the salt and pepper bring out the natural flavor of the scallops. This recipe is perfect for anyone who loves seafood, and it's sure to be a hit with the whole family.

Prep Time: 10 minutes
Cook Time: 5-7 minutes
Servings: 3

Ingredients:

- 1 pound scallops
- 2 tablespoons butter
- 1 tablespoon olive oil
- 1 teaspoon garlic powder

- Salt and pepper to taste

Instructions:

1. Heat a wok over medium-high heat.
2. Add the olive oil and the butter to the pan.
3. When the butter melts, add the scallops to the pan.
4. Sprinkle the garlic powder, salt, and pepper over the scallops.
5. Cook the scallops for 5-7 minutes, flipping them once, until they tur golden brown and cooked through.
6. Serve the scallops immediately and enjoy!

Nutritional information per serving:

Calories: 207 Fats: 15g Carbs: 1g Proteins: 14g

18. Shanghainese-Style Stir-Fried Shrimp

This Shanghainese-style stir-fried shrimp dish is a quick and simple way to enjoy the flavors of Shanghai in your own kitchen. The shrimp cooks quickly in the wok, making this a perfect weeknight meal. Serve it over rice or with steamed vegetables for a complete meal.

Prep Time: 5 minutes
Cook Time: 10 minutes
Servings: 4

Ingredients:

- 1 pound medium-large shrimp, peeled and deveined, tails left on
- 2 tablespoons vegetable oil
- Kosher salt

- 2 teaspoons Shaoxing rice wine
- 2 scallions, finely julienned

Instructions:

1. Using sharp kitchen scissors or a paring knife, slice the shrimp in half lengthwise, keeping the tail section intact. As the shrimp is stir-fried, cutting it this way will give more surface area and create a unique shape and texture!
2. Use paper towels to blot the shrimp dry and keep dry. The drier the shrimp, the more flavorful the dish. You can keep the shrimp refrigerated, rolled up in a paper towel, for up to 2 hours before cooking.
3. Heat a wok on medium-high heat until a drop of water sizzles and evaporates on contact. Pour in the oil and swirl to coat the base of the wok. Season the oil by adding a small pinch of salt, and swirl gently.
4. Add the shrimp all at once to the hot wok. Toss and flip quickly for 2 to 3 minutes, until the shrimp just begins to turn pink. Season with another small pinch of salt, and add the rice wine. Let the wine boil off while you continue stir-frying, about another 2 minutes. The shrimp should separate and curl, still attached at the tail.
5. Placee on a serving platter and garnish with the scallions. Serve hot.

Nutritional information per serving:

Calories: 400 Fats: 18g Carbs: 35g Proteins: 21.1g

19. Wok-Fried Fish with Ginger and Scallions

This fish wok recipe is a simple and delicious way to cook fish. Its sweetness pairs well with the savory soy sauce and ginger, creating a flavorful and satisfying dish. The high heat of the wok cooks the fish quickly, keeping it tender and moist. This recipe is perfect for any meal as it is easy to make and takes less than 20 minutes.

Prep Time: 8 minutes
Cook Time: 14 minutes
Servings: 4

Ingredients:

- 2 oz. white fish fillets (such as tilapia or cod)
- 2 scallions, chopped
- 1 tablespoon minced fresh ginger
- 2 tablespoons soy sauce
- 2 tablespoons vegetable oil

Instructions:

1. Heat a wok or a skillet over high heat. Add the vegetable oil and swirl to coat.
2. Add the scallions and stir-fry for a few seconds until fragrant.
3. Add the ginger and continue to stir-fry for 4 minutes or until they begin to soften.
4. Season the fish fillets with soy sauce and add them to the wok. Cook for 5 minutes on each side or until the fish is cooked through.
5. Serve the fish and ginger mixture over steamed rice or noodles, garnish with chopped fresh cilantro or green onions if desired.

Nutritional information per serving:

Calories 145 Fats: 3.8g Carbs: 20.4g Proteins: 9.4g

20. Wok-Fried Teriyaki Prawns

This recipe is a simple and delicious way to make teriyaki prawns in a wok. The prawns are stir-fried in a mixture of soy sauce, brown sugar, minced garlic, and ground ginger, resulting in a sweet and savory dish with a touch of heat from the ginger. Serve over rice for a complete meal.

Prep Time: 10 minutes
Cook Time: 6 minutes
Servings: 3

Ingredients:

- 1 lb. prawns, peeled and deveined
- ¼ cup soy sauce
- ¼ cup brown sugar
- 2 cloves garlic, minced
- ¼ teaspoon ground ginger

Instructions:

1. In a small bowl, mix minced garlic, soy sauce, brown sugar, and ground ginger together.
2. Heat a wok over high heat.
3. Add the prawns to the wok and stir-fry for 2-3 minutes, until they turn pink and are cooked through.
4. Pour the teriyaki sauce over the prawns and continue to stir-fry for about 3 more minutes, or until the sauce is thick and bubbly.
5. Serve the wok-fried teriyaki prawns over rice and enjoy!

Nutritional information per serving:

Calories: 242 Fats: 10g Carbs: 26g Proteins: 20.2g

21. Balinese Squid

This dish is a quick and easy way to enjoy the flavors of Bali in your own kitchen. The squid is stir-fried with garlic, chili peppers and soy sauce for a balance of spicy, savory and slightly sweet flavors. It's perfect as a main course or as a side dish.

Prep Time: 8 minutes
Cook Time: 6 minutes
Servings: 4

Ingredients:

- 3 lb. squid, cleaned and cut into rings
- 2 cloves of garlic, minced
- 2 red chili peppers, sliced
- 2 tablespoons vegetable oil
- 2 tablespoons soy sauce

Instructions:

1. Add the vegetable oil in a wok over high heat and heat.
2. Add the garlic and chili peppers and stir-fry for 30 seconds.
3. Add the squid to the wok and stir-fry for 2-3 minutes, until it turns opaque.
4. Add the soy sauce and stir-fry for about 2 more minutes.
5. Serve immediately and enjoy!

Nutritional information per serving:

Calories: 100 Fats: 3g Carbs: 6g Proteins: 18g

Chapter 3:

Chicken and Poultry Recipes

22. Chicken Dice Lettuce Wraps

Crunchy and tangy, these Asian-inspired wraps are perfect for a light dinner or when you're looking for a veggie-packed lunch. These wraps are ready to eat in just 10 minutes! Be sure to always have the ingredients on hand to whip up these delicious chicken dice lettuce wraps.

Prep Time: 7 minutes
Cook Time: 10 minutes
Servings: 3

Ingredients:

- 2 lb. boneless, skinless chicken breast, diced
- 1 head lettuce, leaves separated
- 1 red bell pepper, diced
- 2 cloves garlic, minced
- 2 tbsp. soy sauce

Instructions:

1. Add the vegetable oil in a wok over high heat and heat.
2. Add the diced chicken and cook until browned, about 5-7 minutes.
3. Add the diced red bell pepper and minced garlic to the wok. Cook for an additional 2-3 minutes.
4. Pour in the soy sauce and stir everything together until the vegetables are coated and the chicken is cooked through.
5. Serve the chicken mixture in lettuce leaves and enjoy!

Nutritional information per serving:

Calories: 410 Carbs: 40g Fats: 11g Proteins: 33g

23. Kung Pao Chicken

Kung Pao Chicken is a spicy, savory Chinese dish that will surely satisfy your cravings for bold flavors. Whether you're a fan of spicy food or just love the bold flavors of Chinese cuisine, Kung Pao Chicken is a must-try dish that will surely become a new favorite.

Prep Time: 15 minutes
Cook Time: 10 minutes
Servings: 4

Ingredients:

- 1 oz. chicken breasts, boneless, skinless, cut into bite-sized pieces
- 2 tbsp. corn starch
- 2 tbsp. soy sauce
- 2 tbsp. rice vinegar
- 2 tbsp. sesame oil

Instructions:

1. Toss the chicken pieces in a bowl with corn starch.
2. Add the vegetable oil in a wok over high heat and heat. Add sesame oil and once hot, add the chicken.
3. Cook until browned and cooked through or for about 7 minutes.
4. In a small bowl, mix rice vinegar and soy sauce together.
5. Reduce heat to medium-low, add the sauce mixture to the skillet, and stir to coat the chicken.
6. Cook for about 3 more minutes until the sauce thickens.
7. Serve hot over steamed rice. Enjoy!

Nutritional information per serving:

Calories: 382 Carbs: 13g Proteins: 34g Fats: 20g

24. Scrambled Chicken with Hoisin Sauce

Some people like their eggs boiled, others prefer them scrambled. But everyone loves a yummy Chinese dish with a hint of sweet hoisin sauce in it! Like many other Chinese dishes, this one is cooked in just one pot and is easy to make at home.

Prep Time: 10 minutes
Cook Time: 8 minutes
Servings:

Ingredients:

- 1 pound chicken breasts, boneless, skinless, cut into small pieces
- 2 tablespoons vegetable oil
- 3 cloves garlic, minced

- ¼ cup hoisin sauce
- 2 green onions, thinly sliced

Instructions:

1. Add the vegetable oil in a wok over high heat and heat. Swirl to ensure you coat the bottom of the wok.
2. Add the chicken and stir-fry until it is cooked through, about 5 minutes.
3. Add the garlic and stir-fry for 1 more minute, or until fragrant.
4. Stir in the hoisin sauce and cook until the chicken is well coated and heated through, about 2 minutes.
5. Remove the wok from heat and stir in the green onions. Serve hot.

Nutritional information per serving:

Calories: 227 Carbs: 16g Fats: 4g Proteins: 32g

25. Braised Duck in Soy Sauce

Braised Duck in Soy Sauce is a classic Chinese dish that is perfect for a comforting and satisfying meal. The rich, savory flavors of the duck are complemented by the sweet and salty soy sauce, making it a dish that everyone will love. Here is a recipe for making this dish at home using a wok.

Prep Time: 15 minutes
Cook Time: 30 minutes
Servings: 4

Ingredients:

- 1 whole duck, cut into pieces
- ½ cup soy sauce
- ¼ cup sugar
- 2 cloves of garlic, minced
- 2 green onions, sliced

Instructions:

1. Mix the garlic, soy sauce, sugar, and green onions together in a small bowl.
2. Heat a large skillet or a wok on high heat. Add the duck pieces, skin side down, and cook for 6 minutes or until the skin is crispy and golden brown.
3. Flip the duck pieces over and add the soy sauce mixture to the wok. Bring to a boil, lower heat to medium-low and cover the wok.
4. Let the duck simmer in the sauce for 20-25 minutes, or until it is cooked through and tender.
5. Remove the duck pieces from the wok and allow a few minutes to let them cool before slicing and serving.
6. Enjoy this simple and delicious dish!

Note: Keep in mind that this recipe is a basic one and you can adjust ingredients to your own preference. Also it assumes that you already know how to prepare a duck.

Nutritional information per serving:

Calories: 50 Carbs: 4g Fats: 3g Proteins: 5g

26. Turkey Asparagus Stir-Fry

This turkey asparagus stir-fry is a flavorful and easy meal that is perfect for a weeknight dinner. The dish is a great way to incorporate lean Proteins and vegetables in one meal. Serve it over rice or noodles.

Prep Time: 10 minutes
Cook Time: 9 minutes
Servings: 3

Ingredients:

- 1 lb. turkey breast, sliced into thin strips
- 1 bunch of asparagus, trimmed and cut into 1-inch pieces
- 2 cloves of garlic, minced
- 2 tbsp. soy sauce
- 1 tbsp. sesame oil

Instructions:

1. In a small bowl, mix the sesame oil and soy sauce together.
2. Place a wok over high heat and let it heat. Add the turkey to the wok and stir-fry for 3-4 minutes, until cooked through. Remove from the wok and set aside.
3. In the same wok, add the garlic and asparagus and stir-fry for 2-3 minutes, until tender-crisp.
4. Return the turkey to the wok and add the soy sauce mixture. Stir-fry for an additional 1-2 minutes, until everything is well combined and heated through.
5. Serve over noodles or rice, and garnish with green onions or sesame seeds if desired.

Nutritional information per serving:

Calories: 250 Carbs: 5g Fats: 13g Proteins: 27g

27. Glazed Chicken Thighs

This wok-made glazed chicken thighs recipe is a simple and fast way to make a delicious and flavorful meal. It's perfect for a dinner or a casual gathering with friends and family.

Prep Time: 10 minutes
Cook Time: 7 minutes
Servings: 3

Ingredients:

- 8 boneless, skinless chicken thighs
- 2 tablespoons soy sauce
- 1 tablespoon rice vinegar
- 1 tablespoon brown sugar
- 1 teaspoon sesame oil

Instructions:

1. In a small bowl, mix the rice vinegar, soy sauce, brown sugar, and sesame oil together to make the glaze.
2. Place a wok over high heat and let it heat and add the chicken thighs. Cook until they are browned for about 4 minutes on each side.
3. Remove the thighs from the wok and put aside.
4. Pour the glaze into the wok and stir until it begins to bubble.
5. Add the chicken back into the wok and toss to coat with the glaze. Cook for about 2-3 more minutes, or until the chicken is cooked through and the glaze has thickened.
6. Serve the chicken with steamed rice and vegetables, if desired.

Nutritional information per serving:

Calories: 297 Carbs: 5g Fats: 10g Proteins: 46g

28. Chicken with Onion and Pineapple

This recipe is an awesome way to add some excitement to your usual chicken dinner routine. The savory and sweet flavors of the onion and pineapple complement the tender chicken perfectly, and the garlic and ginger add a nice depth of flavor.

Prep Time: 10 minutes
Cook Time: 9 minutes
Servings: 4

Ingredients:

- 1 pound chicken breast, boneless, skinless, cut into bite-sized pieces
- 1 large onion, sliced
- 1 cup pineapple chunks
- 2 tablespoons vegetable oil
- Salt and pepper to taste

Instructions:

1. Place a wok over high heat and let it heat. Add the vegetable oil and swirl to coat the surface.
2. Add the chicken pieces to the wok and stir-fry until they are browned on all sides or for about 3 minutes on each side.
3. Add the sliced onion and stir-fry for an additional 2-3 minutes, or until the onion is lightly browned and soft.
4. Stir in the pineapple chunks and cook for another 2-3 minutes, or until they are heated through.
5. Season the stir-fry with salt and pepper to taste. Serve over rice or noodles if desired.

Nutritional information per serving:

Calories: 290 Carbs: 32g Fats: 12g Proteins: 16g

29. Fiery Pepper Chicken

If you're looking for a little kick, this dish is for you. If spicy food isn't your thing, no worries--I've tried to tone down the pepper just a touch, so it's not too overpowering. I have to say this dish was fairly easy to put together.

Prep Time: 10 minutes
Cook Time: 8 minutes
Servings: 2

Ingredients:

- 8 oz. boneless, skinless chicken breast, cut into bite-sized pieces
- 2 red bell peppers, sliced
- 1 tbsp. oil
- 2 cloves of garlic, minced
- 2 tablespoons of hot sauce

Instructions:

1. Place a wok over high heat and let it heat. Add 1 tablespoon of oil and let it heat.
2. Add chicken and cook for about 3-4 minutes, until browned and cooked through.
3. Add red bell peppers, jalapeño pepper, and garlic to the wok and continue to cook for an additional 2-3 minutes, until vegetables are slightly softened.
4. Stir in the hot sauce and cook for an additional 1-2 minutes to allow the flavors to meld together.
5. Serve hot over rice or noodles.

Nutritional information per serving:

Calories: 190 Fats: 6g Carbs: 10g Proteins: 25g

30. Zucchini Chicken

This dish is a great way to get more vegetables into your diet, and the sauce is so flavorful that it will definitely make your taste buds happy. Plus, this dish can be made in less than 10 minutes, which makes it a great option for busy days. It is also a great dish for those who are looking for a healthy and low-carb option. Give it a try and you will not regret it!

Prep Time: 10 minutes
Cook Time: 9 minutes
Servings: 4

Ingredients:

- 1 pound chicken breast, boneless, skinless, cut into thin strips
- 2 medium zucchini, sliced
- 2 cloves of garlic, minced
- 2 tablespoons olive oil

- 2 tablespoons soy sauce

Instructions:

1. Place a wok over high heat and let it heat. Add the olive oil, and let it get hot.
2. Add the chicken to the pan and stir-fry for 3-5 minutes, or until it is cooked through. Remove the chicken from wok and place it aside.
3. In the same pan, add the zucchini and garlic. Stir-fry for 2-3 minutes, or until the zucchini is tender.
4. Put back the chicken to the wok and add the soy sauce. Toss to coat the chicken and zucchini evenly with the sauce.
5. Cook for an additional 1-2 minutes, until the sauce is heated through and the zucchini is done to your liking.
6. Serve hot with rice or noodles. Enjoy!

Nutritional information per serving:

Calories: 204 Carbs: 3g Fats: 11g Proteins: 20g

31. Homemade Sweet and Sour Chicken

This recipe is perfect for those who love sweet and sour flavors. It can be served over rice and garnished with green onions. This sweet and sour chicken will definitely be a hit at your next dinner party. There's no need for take-out when you can whip up a batch of this restaurant-style dish. This tasty and colorful recipe will give you the same satisfying crunch and hot, spicy flavor as your favorite take-out joint, with only a fraction of the calories.

Prep Time: 5 minutes
Cook Time: 7 minutes
Servings: 2

Ingredients:

- 1 lb. chicken breast, skinless, boneless, cut into bite-sized pieces
- ½ cup corn starch

- ¼ cup flour
- ¼ cup sugar
- 2 tablespoons soy sauce

Instructions:

1. In a shallow dish, mix together the corn-starch and flour. Dredge the chicken pieces in the mixture to coat.
2. In a small saucepan, combine the sugar, rice vinegar, and soy sauce. Cook while stirring occasionally, over medium heat, until the sugar has dissolved.
3. Place a wok over medium-high heat and let it heat and add enough oil to coat the wok's bottom. Once hot, add the chicken pieces and cook for about 3-4 minutes on each side, or until golden brown and cooked through.
4. Add in the sweet and sour sauce over the chicken and stir to coat evenly. Cook for 2-3 more minutes, or until the sauce is thick and the chicken is fully coated.
5. Serve over rice or with your choice of sides and enjoy!

Nutritional information per serving:

Calories: 200 Carbs: 27g Fats: 3g Proteins: 16g

Note: You could adjust the sweetness level of your sauce, you could add pineapple chunks to the sauce for more tropical taste. And also add vegetables like bell peppers, onions, or carrots to the skillet to make it more colorful and nutritious.

32. Chicken and Vegetables

This dish is great for a weekend meal or a weeknight dinner. The combination of fresh vegetables, tender chicken, and flavorful sauce makes for a satisfying and delicious meal. The wok allows for even cooking and a nice char on the vegetables, which adds great flavor and texture to the dish. This recipe is also easily adaptable to include your favorite vegetables or Proteins.

Prep Time: 8 minutes
Cook Time: 12 minutes
Servings: 2

Ingredients:

- 1 oz chicken breast fillets, boneless, skinless, cut into thin strips
- 2 cups mixed vegetables (such as onions, bell peppers, and broccoli)
- 2 cloves of garlic, minced

- 2 tablespoons vegetable oil
- 2 tablespoons soy sauce

Instructions:

1. Place a wok over high heat and let it heat. Add the oil, and let it get hot.
2. To the pan, add the chicken and stir-fry for 3-5 minutes, or until it is cooked through. Set aside the chicken.
3. In the same pan, add the vegetables and garlic. Stir-fry for 3-5 minutes, or until the vegetables are crisp-tender.
4. Place back the chicken to the pan and add the soy sauce. Toss to coat the chicken and vegetables evenly with the sauce.
5. Cook for an additional 1-2 minutes, until the sauce is heated through and the vegetables are done to your liking.
6. Serve hot with rice or noodles. Enjoy!

Nutritional information per serving:

Calories: 325 Carbs: 25g Fats: 14g Proteins: 29g

33. Peanut Chicken Stir-Fry

This dish is a perfect combination of savory and sweet. The peanut butter and soy sauce give it a rich and savory flavor, while the rice vinegar and sesame oil add a nice balance of sweetness and acidity. It is perfect for a quick and easy weeknight dinner. It could also be served over rice or noodles, or even with some added veggies like bell peppers, broccoli, or mushrooms to make it a complete meal

Prep Time: 10 minutes
Cook Time: 7 minutes
Servings: 4

Ingredients:

- 1 pound chicken breasts, boneless, skinless, sliced into thin strips
- ¼ cup creamy peanut butter
- 2 tablespoons soy sauce

- 1 tablespoon rice vinegar
- 1 tablespoon sesame oil

Instructions:

1. In a small bowl, mix the rice vinegar, peanut butter, sesame oil, and soy sauce together to create the stir-fry sauce.
2. In a wok or large skillet, heat a small amount of oil over high heat. Add the sliced chicken and stir-fry for 3-4 minutes, until browned and cooked through.
3. Pour the stir-fry sauce over the chicken and stir to coat. Cook for 2-3 more minutes, until the sauce is thick and the chicken is fully coated.
4. Serve the peanut chicken stir-fry over rice or noodles, garnished with chopped peanuts, green onions, or cilantro if desired.

Nutritional information per serving:

Calories: 307 Carbs: 11g Fats: 20g Proteins: 24g

34. Braised Chicken Wings

Are you looking for something new to try out? braised chicken wings are worth a shot. They are a staple at many restaurants and can be made easily in your own kitchen. You don't have to wait for the summer months for these delicious morsels of poultry and sauce with the ultimate comfort food ingredients: bread, butter, and cream.

Prep Time: 10 minutes
Cook Time: 32 minutes
Servings: 6

Ingredients:

- 2 pounds chicken wings
- 2 cloves garlic, minced
- 1 cup chicken broth
- 2 tablespoons soy sauce
- 2 tablespoons vegetable oil

Instructions:

1. Place a wok over high heat and let it heat.
2. Add the vegetable oil and once hot, add the garlic, stir-fry for 1-2 minutes or until fragrant.
3. Add the chicken wings to the wok and stir-fry for 8-10 minutes or until they are golden brown.
4. Add the chicken broth and soy sauce, bring it to a boil, lower heat to low, cover and let it simmer for 15-20 minutes or until the chicken wings are cooked through.
5. Serve immediately.

Nutritional information per serving:

Calories: 600 Fats: 44g Carbs: 2g Proteins: 40g

Chapter 4:

Rice Recipes

35. Chinese Wok Fried Rice

This Chinese wok fried rice is a quick dish that is perfect for a lunch or dinner. With just a few simple ingredients, this dish is packed with flavor and nutrition. The chicken and vegetables add protein and vitamins, while the soy sauce and sesame oil give the rice a savory and slightly nutty flavor.

Prep Time: 10 minutes
Cook Time: 18 minutes
Servings: 4

Ingredients:

- 2 cups cooked jasmine rice
- 1 cup diced chicken breast
- 1 cup diced vegetables (such as bell peppers, peas, and carrots)
- 2 tablespoons soy sauce
- 1 tablespoon sesame oil

Instructions:

1. Heat a wok over medium-high heat.
2. Add the chicken and vegetables to the wok and stir fry until the vegetables are tender and the chicken is cooked through or for about 8 minutes.
3. Add the already cooked rice to the wok and stir fry for an additional 2-3 minutes.
4. Add in the sesame oil and soy sauce, and cook for about 3 more minutes, or until the rice is evenly covered with the sauce and heated through.
5. Serve hot, garnished with green onions or cilantro if desired.

Nutritional information per serving:

Calories: 239 Proteins: 14g Fats: 7gCarbs: 26g

36. Coconut Rice with Prawns

The Coconut Rice with Prawns Wok recipe is a simple and delicious dish that is perfect for any occasion. The rice is cooked in a flavorful coconut milk and garlic mixture, and then tossed with sautéed prawns for a complete meal.

Prep Time: 15 minutes
Cook Time: 20 minutes
Servings: 4

Ingredients:

- 2 cups of long-grain rice
- 1 can of coconut milk
- 1 pound of large prawns, peeled and deveined
- 2 cloves of garlic, minced
- 2 tablespoons of vegetable oil

Instructions:

1. Put the rice in a bowl with cold water and rinse it thoroughly. Then, add 2 cups of water to a medium saucepan, add the rice and bring to a boil.
2. Lower the heat to low and use a lid to cover the pot. Let the rice simmer until the rice is tender and the water is absorbed or for 18-20 minutes,.
3. While the rice is cooking, place a wok with oil over high heat and let it heat. Add the minced garlic and sauté for 1-2 minutes, until fragrant.
4. Add the prawns to the wok and cook for 2-3 minutes per side, or until they are pink and cooked through.
5. Once the rice is cooked, add the coconut milk and stir well. Cook for 2-3 more minutes, or until the coconut milk is hot and bubbly.
6. Add the cooked prawns to the rice and toss to combine. Serve immediately, garnished with cilantro or green onions if desired.

Nutritional information per serving:

Calories: 480 Proteins: 24g Fats: 18g Carbs: 56g

37. Rice and Grapes Stir Fry

This dish is a favorite of mine. It's a quick, healthy and filling meal that's easy to prepare on a busy work night. It's a perfect one-pan meal with the rice and vegetables cooked together to make it easy on you. The beauty about this dish is that it can be made for practically any occasion.

Prep Time: 15 minutes
Cook Time: 10 minutes
Servings: 4

Ingredients:

- 1 tablespoon vegetable oil
- 1 cup sliced red grapes
- 1 cup cubed cooked chicken
- 2 cups cooked rice
- ¼ cup chicken broth

Instructions:

1. Place a wok with vegetable oil over high heat and let it heat.
2. Stir in the grapes and chicken; cook and stir until the chicken is hot, and the grapes are tender, about 3 minutes.
3. Add the rice and chicken broth; continue cooking for about 2 minutes more, or until the rice is hot.
4. Serve and enjoy

Nutritional information per serving:

Calories: 225.6 Proteins: 8g Carbs: 29.4g Fats: 6.5g

38. Makato's Bacon Fried Rice

This dish is a favorite of many across the world, not just in the east! It's crispy and delicious, will fill your stomach up for real. I highly recommend it for people who want to start their day a little healthier but don't want to give up all that good of fried rice flavor.

Prep Time: 15 minutes
Cook Time: 10 minutes
Servings: 4

Ingredients:

- ½ pound bacon, sliced into small pieces
- 2 tablespoons soy sauce
- 2 medium green onions, chopped
- ¼ teaspoon sea salt
- 2 cups steamed white rice

Instructions:

1. Add the bacon in a wok or large skillet on medium heat and cook, stirring occasionally, until starting to brown, about 5 minutes.
2. Pour in soy sauce and scrape up any brown bits from the bottom of the wok. Add green onions and salt; cook until wilted, 30 seconds to 1 minute.
3. Add rice; cook, stirring frequently, until heated through.
4. Serve and enjoy.

Nutritional information per serving:

Calories: 209.4 Proteins: 9.6g Carbs: 23.7g Fats: 8g

39. Jasmine Rice with Bok Choy

Is your palate looking for something new? Have you been craving a healthy alternative to the same old, same old? Do you have an abundance of bok choy in your fridge, just begging to be paired with something phenomenal that can be made in less than an half hour? Do we have the perfect recipe for you! Learn how to make Jasmine Rice with Bok Choy it's delicious and nutritious, and guaranteed to satisfy any cravings.

Prep Time: 5 minutes
Cook Time: 28 minutes
Servings: 4

Ingredients:

- 1 cup jasmine rice, uncooked
- 1 chopped bok choy head
- 1 tablespoon butter

- 1 tablespoon olive oil
- 2 cups chicken stock

Instructions:

1. Over medium heat, add the butter in a wok and melt it. Add in the bok choy into the wok and stir-fry for about 4 minutes until soft.
2. Add the chicken stock, turn the heat to high and let it boil. Add olive oil, rice and then mix.
3. Lower heat to simmer and use a lid to cover and cook for about 18 minutes. Look to see rice after 9 minutes to ensure that it is cooking well; if the rice overcooks, it will dry, and if it undercooks it will be hard.
4. Serve and enjoy

Nutritional information per serving:

Calories: 246.9 Proteins: 5.3g Carbs: 41.6g Fats: 6.8g

40. Corned Beef Fried Rice with Mint

The delicious corned beef in this dish makes it a little more tenacious than your standard fried rice. It's also much prettier than the dish of mush you find at your local Chinese take-out joint. This version is worthy of a spot on your Thanksgiving table, at least in my opinion.

Prep Time: 10 minutes
Cook Time: 6 minutes
Servings: 2

Ingredients:

- 1 tablespoon olive oil
- 2 cups cooked white rice
- 6 ounces cooked corned beef, thinly sliced
- 1 egg, beaten
- 6 sprig (blank)s fresh spearmint leaves, cut into thin strips

Instructions:

1. Place a wok with olive oil over high heat and let it heat.
2. Cook and stir rice and chicken paste in hot oil until combined, about 2 minutes.
3. Stir corned beef into rice mixture until rice begins to brown, 2 to 4 minutes.
4. Remove the wok from heat and clear a hole in the center of the rice to cook egg.
5. Pour the beaten egg into center of the rice. Tilt the wok around to spread the egg into the rice, allowing the residual heat to completely cook the egg.
6. Portion the fried rice into 2 bowls and top with fresh mint.

Nutritional information per serving:

Calories: 429.7 Proteins: 24.4g Carbs: 46.5g Fats: 15.7g

41. Rice with Bacon

This humble dish, best enjoyed with friends and family, has a long history and significant cultural importance in many societies around the world. It also shares some commonalities with other grain-based dishes. It is a simple dish, requiring only rice and bacon, but rice with bacon can become the centrepiece of any meal.

Prep Time: 5 minutes
Cook Time: 30 minutes
Servings: 4

Ingredients:

- 8oz bacon, cut into small pieces
- 2 tablespoons of soy sauce
- 2 green onions, chopped
- ¼ teaspoon sea salt
- 2 cups of steamed white rice

Instructions:

1. Put the bacon in a wok or a large pan and cook over medium heat for about 5 minutes, stirring occasionally, until it starts to brown.
2. Pour the soy sauce on top and scrape up the brown pieces from the bottom of the wok.
3. Add green onions and salt; Cook for 30 seconds to 1 minute until wilted. Add rice; Cook for 3 to 4 minutes, stirring frequently, until the soy sauce is heated through.

Nutritional information per serving:

Calories: 349 Fats: 1.9g Carbs: 7g Proteins: 3g

42. Pork Fried Rice

Most likely not like anything you've ever seen before, but it's worth a try. Pork fried rice is a dish in which pork and vegetables are mixed with white rice and soy sauce to create an amazing blend of flavors that are lusciously savory. The ingredients stretch your limits and the process surprisingly simple.

Prep Time: 10 minutes
Cook Time: 22 minutes
Servings: 4

Ingredients:

- 1 lb. pork loin, cut into small cubes
- 3 cups white rice, cooked
- 2 tablespoons vegetable oil

- 2 eggs, beaten
- 2 green onions, thinly sliced

Instructions:

1. Place a wok over medium heat and pour in the vegetable oil. Add the pork and stir-fry for about 6 minutes, or until browned and cooked through.
2. Push the pork to the sides of the wok or skillet and add eggs to the center. Scramble the eggs until cooked, then mix them with the pork.
3. Add the cooked rice to the wok or skillet and stir-fry for about 4 minutes or until heated through and well combined with the pork and eggs.
4. Stir in the sliced green onions and continue stir-frying for an additional minute.
5. Serve hot and enjoy your pork fried rice

Nutritional information per serving:

Calories: 420 Proteins: 23g Fats: 16g Carbs: 43g

43. Fried Rice with Lychee

This recipe is a wonderful and easy way to enjoy a classic dish with a unique twist. Cooked white rice is stir-fried with fresh lychee, soy sauce, and vegetable oil for a flavorful and satisfying meal.

Prep Time: 13 minutes
Cook Time: 35 minutes
Servings: 4

Ingredients:

- 1 cup white rice
- 2 cups water
- ¼ cup soy sauce
- 1 cup lychee, peeled and pitted
- ¼ cup vegetable oil

Instructions:

1. Rinse the white rice in a strainer and add it to a pot with water, and bring to boil. Lower heat to low and use a lid to cover the pot. Cook the rice until the rice is soft and the water is absorbed or for about 19 minutes.
2. Place a wok over medium heat and pour in the vegetable oil. Add the already cooked rice to the wok and stir-fry for 4 minutes until the rice is heated through.
3. Add the lychee and soy sauce to the wok and stir-fry for an additional 4 minutes.
4. Serve the fried rice in bowls and enjoy!

Nutritional information per serving:

Calories: 312 Fats: 12g Carbs: 47g Proteins: 4g

44. Wok-Fried Brown Rice

Wok-frying brown rice is a way to cook rice in a wok with little oil or butter. It's got more flavor than steamed or boiled brown rice and can be used in many different dishes. While not everyone has their own wok, many people like to use the non-stick pan for cooking brown rice instead.

Prep Time: 10 minutes
Cook Time: 20 minutes
Servings: 4

Ingredients:

- 2 cups brown rice, rinsed and drained
- 2 tablespoons vegetable oil
- 2 cloves garlic, minced
- 1 teaspoon soy sauce
- ¼ cup frozen peas

Instructions:

1. In a medium saucepan, add water and bring to a boil. Put in the rinsed brown rice and stir.
2. Lower to low heat, cover the pan and simmer for about 20 minutes or until the water is fully absorbed and the rice is cooked.
3. Heat a wok over medium heat. Add the vegetable oil and garlic and stir-fry for 1-2 minutes or until fragrant.
4. Add the cooked brown rice and soy sauce to the wok and stir-fry for 3-5 minutes or until the rice is cooked and well-coated with the sauce.
5. Finally, add the frozen peas and stir-fry for an additional 2-3 minutes or until the peas are heated through.

Nutritional information per serving:

Calories: 288 Fats: 9g Carbs: 48g Proteins: 5g

45. Apple Fried Rice

This is a great dish for breakfast, lunch, or dinner - and it's quick to make too!

Apple fried rice is an elegantly simple dish with a natural sweetness from apples. For a twist on this classic, substitute raisins for the apple slices. This dish has a wonderful taste, and you can use any kind of apple to make it.

Prep Time: 10 minutes
Cook Time: 10 minutes
Servings: 2

Ingredients:

- 1 cup cooked white rice
- 1 red apple, diced
- 2 eggs, beaten

- 2 tablespoons of vegetable oil
- ¼ teaspoon of salt

Instructions:

1. Heat a wok on medium heat.
2. Add the vegetable oil and eggs to the wok, and scramble the eggs until cooked through.
3. Add the diced apple, salt and stir-fry for 2-3 minutes or until the apples are slightly softened.
4. Add the cooked rice and stir-fry until the rice is heated through and the ingredients are well combined.
5. Serve hot and enjoy!

Nutritional information per serving:

Calories: 380 Fats: 19g Carbs: 42g Proteins: 8g

...imp Rice Bowl

...Bowls are a delicious one-pan dish that you can ...n with one pan, which means less time in the kitchen ...ime to enjoy the outdoors. They have a beautiful balance of ...es, with crunchy vegetables on top of soft fried rice topped with ...ispy shrimp and steamed vegetables.

Prep Time: 11 minutes
Cook Time: 15 minutes
Servings: 4

Ingredients:

- 1 lb. shrimp, peeled and deveined
- 2 cups cooked white rice
- 1 cup frozen mixed vegetables (peas, carrots, and corn)
- ¼ cup soy sauce
- ¼ cup oyster sauce

Instructions:

1. Heat a wok on high heat. Add the shrimp and cook for about 3-4 minutes, until pink and slightly charred. Remove the shrimp from the wok and place aside.
2. Add the frozen mixed vegetables to the wok and stir-fry for 2-3 minutes until tender.
3. Mix the oyster sauce and soy sauce together in a small bowl. Add the sauce into the wok and stir to coat the vegetables.
4. Add the already cooked rice to the wok and stir to combine. Cook for another 2-3 minutes until heated through.
5. Put back the cooked shrimp to the wok and stir to combine.
6. Serve the shrimp and vegetable rice mixture in bowls and enjoy!

Nutritional information per serving:

Calories: 267 Fats: 4g Carbs: 33g Proteins: 22g

47. Rice fried with chicken

If you want something more than the same old rice and beans, then switch it up and try rice with chicken! This is an easy recipe that's simple to put together. It's always a good idea to eat a diverse diet. Among the easiest ways to do this is by adding different foods into your regular routine. It's easy to switch out meals or add in new ones when you need something new.

Prep Time: 5 minutes
Cook Time: 30 minutes
Servings: 4

Ingredients:

- 1 pound chicken, cut into small pieces
- 2 tablespoons of soy sauce

- 2 green onions, chopped
- ¼ teaspoon sea salt
- 2 cups steamed white rice

Instructions:

1. Put the chicken in a wok or a large pan and cook over medium heat for about 15 minutes, stirring occasionally, until it cooks through.
2. Pour the soy sauce on top and scrape up the brown pieces from the bottom of the wok. Add green onions and salt; Cook for 30 seconds to 1 minute until wilted. Add rice; Cook for 3 to 4 minutes, stirring frequently, until the soy sauce is heated through.
3. Serve and enjoy.

Nutritional information per serving:

Calories: 349 Fats: 1.9g Carbs: 7g Proteins: 3g

48. Fried rice with duck

Fried rice is an amazing dish, whether you make it from scratch or use a packet mix. One type of fried rice that is worth mentioning is a mixture of sticky rice, duck, and vegetables. It's very light in flavor, and the flavors all work together incredibly well for such a simple dish.

Prep Time: 15 minutes
Cook Time: 35 minutes
Servings: 4

Ingredients:

- 1 cup minced Chinese roast duck, skin and fats removed and set aside
- 6 green onions, thinly sliced
- 2 tablespoons of soy sauce
- 3 cups cooked long grain rice
- Salt to taste

Instructions:

1. Heat a large pan or wok on medium heat and add the duck skin and Fats. Fry the duck skin and Fats for about 10 minutes until the Fats has melted and the duck skin is crispy.
2. Raise the temperature to medium to high heat, then add the duck. Also add about half of the green onions and the soy sauce. Keep cooking and stirring until the meat is cooked through.
3. This should take about 5 minutes - Add rice. Add the rice and stir for 5 minutes until the rice sizzles and is hot. Divide the rice in half and make a wide indentation in the rice so that the bottom of the wok is exposed.
4. Add the remaining green onions quickly start mixing!
5. Continue stirring for 5 minutes or until the rice is very hot. Season with salt and serve.

Nutritional information per serving:

Calories: 368 Fats: 5.1 Carbs: 1.3 Proteins: 4.6

49. Garlic Fried Rice

Fried rice is a delicious, healthy way to start the day. When you add garlic, it makes a meal that's even better! But let's be honest. If you've ever tried to make savory fried rice the traditional way, you'll know that it's not always easy to get the right amount of crispiness. This homemade recipe is a little bit healthier than your usual fried rice, but no less tasty!

Prep Time: 7 minutes
Cook Time: 14 minutes
Servings: 3

Ingredients:

- 2 cups cooked white rice
- 3 cloves of garlic, minced
- 2 eggs
- 2 green onions, sliced

- 2 tablespoons vegetable oil

Instructions:

1. Place a wok over high heat and let it heat and add the oil. Let the oil heat up.
2. Crack the eggs into the wok and scramble until cooked through. Remove from the wok and set aside.
3. Add the minced garlic to the wok and stir-fry for 3 minutes until fragrant.
4. Add the rice and stir to combine with the garlic. Cook for 2-3 minutes until heated through.
5. Add the scrambled eggs and green onions and stir to combine.
6. Serve the garlic fried rice in bowls and enjoy!

Nutritional information per serving:

Calories: 239 Fats: 9g Carbs: 32g Proteins: 6g

Chapter 5:

Noodles Recipes

50. Garlic Noodles

This dish is perfect for those who love garlic and noodles. The dish is simple and easy to make, with a great balance of savory flavors. Enjoy the Garlic Noodles with your favorite Asian-inspired meal or as a side dish.

Prep Time: 10 minutes
Cook Time: 2 minutes
Servings: 2

Ingredients:

- 8 oz. dried Chinese egg noodles or spaghetti
- 3 garlic cloves, minced
- 2 tbsp. vegetable oil
- Salt, to taste
- 2 tbsp. chopped green onions (optional)

Instructions:

1. Cook the noodles as per the instructions on the package, then drain and set aside.
2. Place a wok over high heat and let it heat. Add the vegetable oil.
3. Add the minced garlic and stir-fry for about 30 seconds, or until fragrant. Be careful not to burn the garlic.
4. Add the noodles to the wok and stir-fry for about 2 minutes, or until the noodles are heated through and well coated in the garlic and oil.
5. Season with salt to taste and stir in the green onions, if using. Serve immediately.

Nutritional information per serving:

Calories: 315 | Carbs: 1g | Fats: 0g | Proteins: 6g

51. Wok Buttered Peanut Noodles

Wok Buttered Peanut Noodles is a classic Chinese dish that's easy to make and scrumptious. Add veggies and chicken for even more flavor. Check out this recipe today! It's super easy to put together and totally delicious.

Prep Time: 10 minutes
Cook Time: 5 minutes
Servings: 3

Ingredients:

- 8 oz. spaghetti or rice noodles
- ¼ cup creamy peanut butter
- 2 tbsp. butter
- 2 cloves of garlic, minced
- 2 tbsp. soy sauce

Instructions:

1. Cook the spaghetti or rice noodles according to package instructions. Drain and set aside.
2. Add the butter to a wok or large skillet on medium heatand melt it. Add the minced garlic and cook for 1-2 minutes, until fragrant.
3. Stir in the peanut butter and soy sauce until well combined.
4. Add in the noodles to the wok and toss to coat in the sauce. Cook for an additional 2-3 minutes, until heated through.
5. Serve hot and enjoy!

Nutritional information per serving:

Calories: 421 Fats: 22g Carbs: 43g Proteins: 12g

Note: You can add vegetables like broccoli, bell pepper, snap peas to make it more nutritious.

52. Glass Noodles with Green Beans and Napa Cabbage

This dish is a great option for anyone looking for a quick and easy meal that is packed with flavor and nutrition. The glass noodles provide a satisfying chewy texture, while the green beans and Napa cabbage add a nice crunch. The soy sauce and garlic give the dish a savory and slightly sweet flavor that is sure to please the whole family.

Prep Time: 6 minutes
Cook Time: 8 minutes
Servings: 3

Ingredients:

- 8 oz. glass noodles
- ½ lb. green beans, trimmed
- ¼ head Napa cabbage, thinly sliced

- 2 cloves garlic, minced
- ¼ cup soy sauce

Instructions:

1. Soak the noodles for 10-15 minutes in warm water, or until they are translucent and pliable. Drain the noodles and set them aside.
2. Add salted water pot and bring to a boil and blanch the green beans for 2-3 minutes, or until they are bright green and tender. Drain the green beans and run them under cold water to cool them down.
3. Place a wok over high heat and let it heat and add a drizzle of oil. Add the garlic and stir-fry for half a minute, or until fragrant.
4. Add the Napa cabbage and stir-fry for 1-2 minutes, or until it starts to wilt.
5. Add the green beans, glass noodles, and soy sauce to the skillet and stir-fry for another 2-3 minutes, or until everything is heated through and well coated with the sauce. Serve hot.

Nutritional information per serving:

Calories: 70 Carbs: 5g Fats: 0g Proteins: 1g

53. Gravy with Shrimp and Rice Noodles

If you are looking for a simple, easy to make or take-to-work dinner to complement your shrimp and rice noodles, here is one that might be perfect for you. This recipe is low in Fats and high in Proteins. This recipe is a classic Thai one. It's a delicious, wholesome meal that doesn't take long to make.

This recipe is vegetarian and gluten-free but can also easily be adapted with adding other ingredients such as onion and carrots into the sauce while simmering on the stovetop.

Prep Time: 10 minutes
Cook Time: 4 minutes
Servings: 3

Ingredients:

- 8 oz. thin egg noodles

- 2 tablespoons olive oil
- 2 cloves of garlic, minced
- ¼ cup cilantro, chopped
- ¼ cup scallions, thinly sliced

Instructions:

1. Prepare the noodles as per the package instructions, then drain and set aside.
2. Place a wok over high heat and let it heat. Add olive oil and heat for 2 minutes.
3. Add garlic and cook for about 1-2 minutes, until fragrant.
4. Add the already cooked noodles to the wok and toss everything together until well combined.
5. Stir in cilantro and scallions, and cook for an additional 1-2 minutes to allow the flavors to meld together.
6. Serve hot and garnish with more cilantro and scallions if desired.

Nutritional information per serving:

Calories: 314 Carbs: 47g Proteins: 8g Fats: 11g

54. Hakka Noodles

Hakka Noodles, also known as "chow mein" in Cantonese, is a popular dish in Chinese cuisine that originated from the Hakka people. It is made with thin wheat flour noodles and a variety of vegetables and meats. This wok-made recipe is perfect for a quick and easy lunch or dinner.

Prep Time: 5 minutes
Cook Time: 5 minutes
Servings: 3

Ingredients:

- 8 oz. Hakka noodles
- ¼ cup soy sauce
- 2 cloves garlic, minced
- ½ cup chopped cabbage

- ½ cup diced carrots

Instructions:

1. Cook the Hakka noodles in boiling water according to package instructions, drain and set aside.
2. In a wok, heat a drizzle of oil over medium-high heat. Add the garlic and stir-fry for half a minute, or until fragrant.
3. Add the diced carrots and stir-fry for 2-3 minutes or until they begin to soften.
4. Add the chopped cabbage, stir-fry for 1-2 minutes or until it starts to wilt.
5. Add the cooked noodles and soy sauce, toss well until everything is heated through and well coated with the sauce. Serve hot.

Nutritional information per serving:

Calories: 260 Carbs: 56g Fats: 1g Proteins: 8g

55. Satay Veggie Noodles

For those who love a good noodle and a healthy dose of vegetables, this recipe is for you! The Satay Vegetable Noodle dish is a vegan, gluten-free option that tastes great with satay marinade or stir-fry sauce. This is a really easy recipe to get through and very tasty.

Prep Time: 10 minutes
Cook Time: 4 minutes
Servings: 2

Ingredients:

- 8 oz. thin rice noodles
- 2 cups mixed vegetables, sliced (such as bell peppers, carrots, and onions)
- 2 tablespoons satay sauce
- 2 tablespoons soy sauce
- 2 tablespoons peanuts, chopped

Instructions:

1. Prepare the rice noodles as per the package instructions, then drain and set aside.
2. Place a wok over high heat and let it heat, add 1 tablespoon of oil and heat.
3. Add mixed vegetables and cook for about 3-4 minutes, until slightly softened.
4. In a small bowl, mix together satay sauce and soy sauce. Add the mixture to the wok, and stir to coat the vegetables.
5. Add the already cooked noodles to the wok and toss everything together until well combined.
6. Garnish with chopped peanuts before serving.

Nutritional information per serving:

Calories: 329 Proteins: 8g Fats: 7g Carbs: 62g

56. Broccoli and Beef Noodles

This recipe is one of the most popular among Chinese home cooks. It can be served as a noodle soup, or a dry preparation that is stir-fried with oil and salt. It is a dish that is very low in calories, and can be prepared with a variety of ingredients to suit your nutritional needs.

Prep Time: 10 minutes
Cook Time: 7 minutes
Servings: 2

Ingredients:

- 8 oz. beef sirloin, sliced into thin strips
- 2 cups broccoli florets
- 8 oz. thin egg noodles
- 2 tablespoons oyster sauce
- 1 tablespoon vegetable oil

Instructions:

1. Prepare the egg noodles as per package instructions, then drain and put aside.
2. Place a wok over medium-high heat and let it heat. Add 1 tablespoon of oil and heat.
3. Add beef and cook for about 3-4 minutes, until browned and cooked through.
4. Add broccoli florets and continue to cook for an additional 2-3 minutes, until vegetables are slightly softened.
5. Add the oyster sauce to the wok, and stir to coat the beef and vegetables.
6. Add the already cooked noodles to the wok and toss everything together until well combined.
7. Serve hot and garnish with green onions or sesame seeds if desired.

Nutritional information per serving:

Calories: 460 Proteins: 30g Fats: 12g Carbs: 53g

57. Dan Dan Noodles

Dan Dan Noodles is a classic Sichuan dish that is known for its spicy, savory, and slightly sweet flavor profile. This recipe is made using a wok for maximum flavor and is perfect for a quick and easy weeknight dinner.

Prep Time: 5 minutes
Cook Time: 10 minutes
Servings: 2

Ingredients:

- 8 oz. fresh or dried Chinese egg noodles
- ¼ cup Sesame paste
- 2 cloves of garlic, minced
- ¼ cup soy sauce
- ¼ cup ground pork or beef

Instructions:

1. Prepare the egg noodles as per package instructions, then drain and put aside.
2. In a small pan, brown the ground pork or beef over medium-high heat, breaking it up as it cooks. Drain off any excess Fats and set aside.
3. In a wok or large skillet, heat a drizzle of oil over medium-high heat. Add the minced garlic and stir-fry for a few seconds until fragrant.
4. Add the browned meat and stir-fry until well combined with garlic.
5. Add the cooked noodles, sesame paste, and soy sauce and stir-fry until the sauce is well distributed. Serve hot with a sprinkle of Szechuan peppercorns or chili flakes for an extra kick.

Nutritional information per serving:

Calories: 146 Carbs: 17g Fats: 7g Proteins: 4g

Note: Dan-Dan Noodles is a classic Sichuanese dish with a strong, savory and spicy flavor, you can adjust the spice level according to your taste by adding more or less of chili oil or chili flakes, or change the Proteins for more option. Topped with green onions and cilantro.

58. Coriander with Pork Noodles

This dish combines the fragrant and flavorful herb coriander (also known as cilantro) with tender pork and noodles. The dish is seasoned with a combination of savory ingredients.

Prep Time: 10 minutes
Cook Time: 12 minutes
Servings: 4

Ingredients:

- 8 oz. spaghetti or rice noodles
- 1 lb. boneless pork loin, thinly sliced
- ¼ cup chopped fresh coriander
- 2 cloves of garlic, minced
- 2 tbsp. soy sauce

Instructions:

1. Cook the spaghetti or rice noodles according to package instructions. Drain and set aside.
2. In a large skillet or a wok, add the pork over medium-high heat and cook for about 5-6 minutes or until its cook through.
3. Add in the garlic and cook for one more minute, or until fragrant.
4. Add in the soy sauce and cook while stirring for another 1-2 minutes.
5. Add the cooked noodles and chopped coriander to the wok, toss to coat in the sauce. Cook for an additional 2-3 minutes, until heated through.
6. Serve hot and enjoy!

Nutritional information per serving:

Calories: 446 Fats: 16g Carbs: 42g Proteins: 3 g

59. Chinese Birthday Noodles

Chinese Birthday Noodles are a traditional dish that is often served on birthdays as a symbol of longevity and good luck. This recipe is made using a wok, and is a simple and delicious way to celebrate any birthday.

Prep Time: 8 minutes
Cook Time: 4 minutes
Servings: 2

Ingredients:

- 8 oz. fresh Chinese egg noodles
- 2 tbsp. vegetable oil
- 2 cloves of garlic, minced
- 2 green onions, thinly sliced
- 2 tbsp. soy sauce

Instructions:

1. Prepare the Chinese egg noodles as per package instructions, then drain and put aside.
2. Place a wok over high heat and let it heat. Add the vegetable oil and swirl to coat the bottom of the wok.
3. Add the garlic and green onions, and stir-fry for about 30 seconds, until fragrant.
4. Add the already-cooked noodles to the wok and stir-fry for 1-2 minutes, until the noodles are heated through.
5. Stir in the soy sauce and continue to stir-fry for another 1-2 minutes, until the noodles are well coated and the sauce is heated through.
6. Serve immediately and enjoy!

Nutritional information per serving:

Calories: 100 Carbs: 16g Fats: 1g Proteins: 7g

Note: This recipe is basic and you can add any vegetable or Proteins of your preference, like mushroom, Bok choy, shrimp, beef or chicken, be creative!

60. Saucy Thai Beef Noodles

This saucy Thai beef noodles dish is a perfect balance of sweet, savory and spicy. This dish is a perfect balance of flavors and will be enjoyed by everyone. It's a perfect recipe for a quick and easy weeknight dinner.

Prep Time: 10 minutes
Cook Time: 11 minutes
Servings: 3

Ingredients:

- 8 oz. rice noodles
- 1 lb. beef sirloin, sliced into thin strips
- 2 cloves of garlic, minced
- ¼ cup Thai sweet chili sauce
- 2 tbsp. soy sauce

Instructions:

1. Prepare the rice noodles as per package instructions, then drain and put aside.
2. Place a wok over high heat and let it heat. Add the beef to the wok and stir-fry for 3-4 minutes, until browned.
3. Add the garlic to the wok and stir-fry for an additional 1-2 minutes, until fragrant.
4. Stir in the Thai sweet chili sauce and soy sauce and bring to a simmer. Cook for about 3 minutes, until the sauce thickens.
5. Add the already cooked rice noodles to the wok and toss to coat with the sauce. Cook for an additional 1-2 minutes, until everything is heated through.
6. Serve the saucy Thai beef noodles in bowls and garnish with fresh cilantro or chopped peanuts if desired.

Nutritional information per serving:

Calories: 536 Carbs: 58g Fats: 19g Proteins: 34g

61. Chicken Stir Fry Noodles

This quick and easy chicken stir fry noodle dish is fully-loaded with vegetables, protein, and a flavorful sauce that's sure to satisfy your craving. It's also vegan so you don't have to feel guilty about indulging in this one! This dinner is perfect for busy weeknights or as a light lunch. It's quick, easy, and full of flavor.

Prep Time: 10 minutes
Cook Time: 7 minutes
Servings: 2

Ingredients:

- 8 oz. boneless, skinless chicken breast, sliced into thin strips
- 8 oz. stir-fry noodles
- 1 red bell pepper, sliced
- ¼ cup soy sauce
- 1 tbsp. vegetable oil

Instructions:

1. Cook stir-fry noodles according to package instructions, then drain and place aside.
2. In a wok, heat 1 tablespoon of oil over medium-high heat.
3. Add chicken and cook for about 3-4 minutes, until browned and cooked through.
4. Add red bell pepper and continue to cook for an additional 2-3 minutes, until vegetables are slightly softened.
5. Add soy sauce to the wok, and stir to coat the chicken and vegetables.
6. Add the already cooked noodles to the wok and toss everything together until well combined.
7. Serve and enjoy your meal.

Nutritional information per serving:

Calories: 397 Proteins: 25g Fats: 12g Carbs: 47g

62. Long Life Noodles

Long life noodles, also known as longevity noodles or yi mein, are a traditional Chinese dish often served at special occasions such as birthdays and weddings. The noodles are typically served in a broth. The name "long life noodles" is derived from the fact that they are symbolically eaten to represent a long and healthy life. They are also considered good luck and prosperity.

Prep Time: 10 minutes
Cook Time: 10 minutes
Servings: 2

Ingredients:

- 8 oz. Chinese egg noodles
- 2 tablespoons oyster sauce
- 2 cloves of garlic, minced
- ¼ cup green onions, sliced

- 1 tbsp. sesame oil

Instructions:

1. Prepare the Chinese egg noodles as per package instructions, then drain and put aside.
2. In a wok, heat 1 tablespoon of oil over medium-high heat.
3. Add garlic and cook for about 1-2 minutes, until fragrant.
4. Add oyster sauce, and the cooked noodles to the wok and toss everything together until well combined.
5. Cook for an additional 1-2 minutes to allow the flavors to meld together.
6. Garnish with green onions before serving.

Nutritional information per serving:

Calories: 456 Proteins: 14g Fats: 3g Carbs: 93g

63. Sesame with Soy Sauce Noodles

Sesame with soy sauce noodles is a traditional Chinese dish made with egg noodles, sesame paste, and soy sauce. The dish is usually served cold and is a popular summertime dish.

Prep Time: 10 minutes
Cook Time: 10 minutes
Servings: 2

Ingredients:

- 8 oz. thin egg noodles
- 2 tablespoons soy sauce
- 2 tablespoons sesame oil
- 2 tablespoons sesame seeds
- 2 green onions, thinly sliced

Instructions:

1. Prepare the egg noodles as per package instructions, then drain and put aside.
2. In a wok or large skillet, heat sesame oil over medium-high heat.
3. Add the prepared noodles to the wok and toss everything together until well combined.
4. Stir in soy sauce, sesame seeds and green onions, and cook for an additional 1-2 minutes to allow the flavors to meld together.
5. Serve hot and garnish with more sesame seeds and green onions if desired.

Nutritional information per serving:

Calories: 309 Proteins: 8g Fats: 10g Carbs: 47g

64. Sirloin Stir-Fry with Ramen Noodles

This dish is an incredibly delicious, cheap, and easy option for a weeknight meal. The sirloin beef with its rich beef flavor and the salty soy sauce provide a satisfying taste perfect for those nights when you just want to curl up in bed after dinner.

Prep Time: 10 minutes
Cook Time: 8 minutes
Servings: 2

Ingredients:

- 8 oz. beef sirloin, sliced into thin strips
- 2 cups mixed vegetables, sliced (such as bell peppers, carrots, and onions)
- 2 packs of ramen noodles, seasoning packets discarded
- 2 tablespoons soy sauce
- 2 tablespoons sesame oil

Instructions:

1. Prepare the egg noodles as per package instructions, then drain and put aside. Discard the seasoning packets.
2. In a wok, heat 1 tablespoon of oil over medium-high heat.
3. Add beef and cook for about 3-4 minutes, until browned and cooked through.
4. Add mixed vegetables and continue to cook for an additional 2-3 minutes, until vegetables are slightly softened.
5. Stir in soy sauce and sesame oil, and cook for an additional 1-2 minutes to allow the flavors to meld together.
6. Add the cooked ramen noodles to the wok and toss everything together until well combined.
7. Serve hot and garnish with green onions or sesame seeds if desired.

Nutritional information per serving:

Calories: 532 Proteins: 30g Fats: 23g Carbs: 51g

65. Cilantro with Scallions Noodles

This Cilantro with Scallions Noodles recipe is a delicious and easy dish that can be made in just a few minutes. It is a good way to use up any leftover noodles you may have in the fridge and is a great way to add some flavor to your meals.

Prep Time: 7 minutes
Cook Time: 4 minutes
Servings: 2

Ingredients:

- 8 oz. thin egg noodles
- 2 tablespoons olive oil
- 2 cloves of garlic, minced
- ¼ cup cilantro, chopped
- ¼ cup scallions, thinly sliced

Instructions:

1. Prepare the egg noodles as per package instructions, then drain and put aside.
2. In a wok, heat olive oil over high heat.
3. Add garlic and cook for about 1-2 minutes, until fragrant.
4. Add the prepared noodles to the wok and toss everything together until well combined.
5. Stir in cilantro and scallions, and cook for an additional 1-2 minutes to allow the flavors to meld together.
6. Serve hot and garnish with more cilantro and scallions if desired.

Nutritional information per serving:

Calories: 314 Proteins: 8g Fats: 11g Carbs: 47g

Chapter 6:

Beef, Pork and Lamb Recipes

66. Gingered Beef with Broccoli

This Gingered Beef with Broccoli recipe is a hearty dish that is ideal for a hungry stomach. It is a great way to add some Asian flavors to your dining table and is sure to please all the eaters. This recipe is suitable for any occasion and will leave your guests satisfied and happy.

Prep Time: 8 minutes
Cook Time: 9 minutes
Servings: 4

Ingredients:

- 12 lb. flank steak, thinly sliced
- 2 heads broccoli, cut into florets
- ¼ cup soy sauce
- 2 tbsp. grated ginger
- 2 tbsp. vegetable oil

Instructions:

1. In a bowl, mix together soy sauce, grated ginger, and 1 tablespoon of vegetable oil. Add the beef and toss to coat. Marinate for at least 20 minutes.
2. Heat a large wok over high heat. Add the remaining tablespoon of oil and once hot, add the beef and cook for about 3 minutes per side or until browned and cooked through.
3. Remove the beef from skillet and set aside.
4. Add broccoli florets to the skillet and stir fry for 2-3 minutes or until slightly tender.
5. Return the cooked beef to the skillet with broccoli and toss to combine.
6. Serve immediately over steamed rice.

Nutritional information per serving:

Calories: 263 Carbs: 10g Fats: 10g Proteins: 31g

67. Lamb with Gingered Scallions

This recipe is a simple, flavorful stir-fry dish made with lamb and ginger scallions. It is a quick and easy meal perfect for a busy weeknight dinner. The ginger and scallions give a perfect balance of flavor to the dish, and the soy sauce and rice wine/sherry helps bring out all the flavors of the lamb.

Prep Time: 7 minutes
Cook Time: 15 minutes
Servings: 4

Ingredients:

- 1 lb. lamb, cut into bite-sized pieces
- 2 tbsp. soy sauce
- 2 tbsp. rice wine (or dry sherry)
- 1 tbsp. grated ginger
- 4 scallions, thinly sliced on an angle

Instructions:

1. In a bowl, mix together the grated ginger, rice wine, and soy sauce. Add the lamb and toss to coat. Marinate for at least 20 minutes.
2. Heat a large wok over high heat. Remove the lamb from the marinade and reserve the marinade.
3. Once hot, add the lamb to the wok and stir-fry for 5 minutes until browned and cooked through.
4. Add the scallions to the wok and stir-fry for another 10 minutes.
5. Finally, pour in the reserved marinade, and stir until the sauce thickens and coats the lamb and scallions. Serve over steamed rice.

Nutritional information per serving:

Calories: 340 Carbs: 11g Fats: 12g Proteins: 34g

68. Pork with Mushrooms

This is an easy, flavorful, and quick Chinese style stir-fry dish. The pork and mushrooms are stir-fried together with a savory oyster sauce, it's a perfect weeknight meal that comes together quickly, and the oyster sauce gives the dish a rich and savory flavor with the added benefits of the mushrooms.

Prep Time: 10 minutes
Cook Time: 9 minutes
Servings: 3

Ingredients:

- 1 oz pork tenderloin, cut into bite-sized pieces
- 8 oz. sliced mushrooms (shiitake, cremini, or button)
- 2 cloves of garlic, minced
- 2 tbsp. oyster sauce
- 1 tbsp. corn starch

Instructions:

1. In a bowl, mix together the corn starch and oyster sauce. Add the pork and toss to coat. Marinate for at least 20 minutes.
2. Heat a large wok over high heat. Once hot, add the pork and stir-fry for 3-5 minutes until browned and well-cooked. Remove from the wok and place aside.
3. In the same wok, add sliced mushrooms and stir-fry for 2-3 minutes until they release their moisture and start to brown.
4. Add the minced garlic and stir-fry for another 30 seconds.
5. Return the pork to the wok, and add the marinade, stir until the sauce thickens and coats the pork and mushrooms.
6. Serve hot over steamed rice.

Nutritional information per serving:

Calories: 327 Carbs: 6g Fats: 16g Proteins: 32g

69. Sichuan Pork with Peanuts

This recipe is a popular dish in Sichuan Chinese cuisine, typically characterized by its numbing heat from Sichuan peppercorn, and it is a easy way to make it at home. The peanuts add a delicious crunchy texture and a great way to balance out the spiciness.

Prep Time: 15 minutes
Cook Time: 8 minutes
Servings: 4

Ingredients:

- 1 lb. pork tenderloin, thinly sliced
- ¼ cup Sichuan peppercorns, toasted and ground
- 2 tbsp. soy sauce
- 2 tbsp. sugar
- ½ cup roasted peanuts

Instructions:

1. In a bowl, mix together the ground Sichuan peppercorns, soy sauce, and sugar. Add the sliced pork and toss to coat. Marinate for at least 20 minutes.
2. Place a wok over high heat and let it heat. Once hot, add the marinated pork and stir-fry for 3-5 minutes until browned and cooked through.
3. Add the roasted peanuts to the wok and stir-fry for another 2-3 minutes.
4. Serve hot over steamed rice.

Nutritional information per serving:

Calories: 375 Carbs: 21g Fats: 18g Proteins: 28g

70. Cardamom Beef Rendang Wok

This recipe is characterized by its rich, complex flavors, with a balance of sweet, savory, and slightly spicy. It is a slow-cooking dish with beef braised in coconut milk, a combination of spices and tamarind paste. The use of cardamom in this recipe gives a unique and warm fragrance to the dish, and make it stand out. It's a great selection if you want to make something flavorful but also have time for a long-cooking dish.

Prep Time: 10 minutes
Cook Time: 1 hour
Servings: 3

Ingredients:

- 1 lb. beef chuck, cut into bite-sized pieces
- 2 cans of coconut milk

- 2 tbsp. tamarind paste
- 2 tbsp. palm sugar
- 2 tsp. ground cardamom

Instructions:

1. In a bowl, mix together the ground cardamom, tamarind paste, and palm sugar.
2. Place a wok over high heat and let it heat, add the beef chunks, and brown them for a few minutes, then pour in the coconut milk and the mixed paste, bring it to a simmer.
3. Lower the heat to low, cover, and let it cook for about an 60 minutes or till the beef is tender and the sauce is thick.
4. Before serving, adjust the seasoning to taste by adding more sugar or tamarind paste if needed.
5. Serve with steamed rice, and garnish with chopped fresh cilantro.

Nutritional information per serving:

Calories: 628 Carbs: 29g Fats: 30g Proteins: 57g

71. Adobo Lamb with Cabbage

This recipe is an adaptation of the Filipino classic dish "adobo" which is traditionally made with pork or chicken. In this recipe we use lamb meat to have a different taste and add cabbage to have a different texture.

Prep Time: 15 minutes
Cook Time: 7 minutes
Servings: 3

Ingredients:

- 2 lb. lamb shoulder, cut into bite-sized pieces
- ¼ cup soy sauce
- 2 cloves garlic, minced
- 1 tbsp. brown sugar
- ½ head of green cabbage, shredded

Instructions:

1. In a bowl, mix together the brown sugar, minced garlic, and soy sauce. Add the lamb and toss to coat. Marinate for at least 20 minutes.
2. Place a wok over high heat and let it heat. Once hot, add the marinated lamb and stir-fry for 3-5 minutes until browned and cooked through.
3. Add the shredded cabbage to the wok and stir-fry for another 2-3 minutes.
4. Serve hot as a side dish or over steamed rice.

Nutritional information per serving:

Calories: 443 Carbs: 31g Fats: 14g Proteins: 34g

72. Sweet-and-Sour Beef Wok Stir-Fry

This sweet and sour beef stir-fry is a delicious and easy meal that is perfect for a weeknight dinner. The tender beef is stir-fried with pineapple in a sweet and sour sauce and red bell pepper that is sure to please everyone. It can be served over rice or noodles for a complete meal.

Prep Time: 10 minutes
Cook Time: 10 minutes
Servings: 4

Ingredients:

- 1 lb. beef sirloin, sliced into thin strips
- 1 red bell pepper, sliced
- 1 cup pineapple chunks

- ¼ cup sweet and sour sauce
- 1 tbsp. corn-starch

Instructions:

1. In a small bowl, mix together the sweet and sour sauce and cornstarch until well combined.
2. Place a wok over high heat and let it heat. Add the beef to the wok and stir-fry for 3-4 minutes, until browned.
3. Add the red bell pepper and pineapple chunks to the wok and stir-fry for an additional 2-3 minutes, until the vegetables are tender-crisp.
4. Add in the sweet and sour sauce mixture and stir-cook for 2-3 minutes, until the sauce thickens.
5. Serve the stir-fry over rice or noodles.

Nutritional information per serving:

Calories: 155 Carbs: 26g Fats: 12g Proteins: 19g

73. Gingered Lamb with Green Beans

This recipe can be adjusted to personal taste by adjusting the amount of ginger or soy sauce as per your liking. You can also add a tablespoon of vegetable oil or sesame oil for additional flavor.

Prep Time: 15 minutes
Cook Time: 7 minutes
Servings: 3

Ingredients:

- 1 lb. lamb, thinly sliced
- 1 tbsp. grated ginger
- 2 cloves of garlic, minced
- ¼ cup soy sauce
- 1 lb. green beans, trimmed

Instructions:

1. In a small bowl, mix the garlic, ginger, and soy sauce together.
2. Place a wok over high heat and let it heat. Once hot, add the lamb and cook for 3-4 minutes, until browned on the outside but still pink in the middle.
3. Remove the lamb from the wok and set aside.
4. Place the green beans to the wok and stir-fry for 2-3 minutes, until they start to soften.
5. Return the lamb to the wok and add the soy sauce mixture. Toss everything together until the lamb and green beans are well coated and the lamb is cooked through.
6. Serve immediately and enjoy!

Nutritional information per serving:

Calories: 327 Carbs: 15g Fats: 15g Proteins: 33g

74. Beef and Zucchini Stir-Fry

This recipe is a great way to incorporate more vegetables into your diet while still getting a good amount of Proteins. The thin slices of beef cook quickly and the zucchinis add a nice crunch to the dish. The combination of soy sauce, oil, and garlic give the dish a savory and slightly sweet flavor.

Prep Time: 15 minutes
Cook Time: 10 minutes
Servings: 4

Ingredients:

- 1 lb. beef sirloin, thinly sliced

- 3 medium zucchinis, cut into bite-sized pieces
- 2 cloves of garlic, minced
- 2 tbsp. vegetable oil
- 2 tbsp. soy sauce

Instructions:

1. Place a wok over high heat and let it heat. Add 1 tablespoon of oil and the beef and cook, stirring occasionally, until browned, about 5 minutes. Remove beef from the wok and place aside.
2. Add the garlic and the remaining 1 tablespoon of oil to the wok. Cook for 30 seconds, until fragrant.
3. Add the zucchinis to the wok and stir-fry for 2-3 minutes, until just starting to soften.
4. Add back the beef to the wok and add the soy sauce. Stir-fry for 1-2 minutes more, until the beef is cooked through and the zucchinis are tender but still crisp.
5. Serve immediately, garnished with cilantro or green onions if desired.

Nutritional information per serving:

Calories: 150 Carbs: 49g Fats: 7g Proteins: 17g

Note: You can also add vegetables like bell peppers, mushrooms or onions for more flavor. Feel free to adjust the amount of soy sauce to taste.

75. Ginger Meat

This dish is a quick and easy stir-fry that is packed with flavor. The combination of ginger and garlic gives the meat a delicious and aromatic taste, while the soy sauce adds a hint of saltiness.

Prep Time: 5 minutes
Cook Time: 5 minutes
Servings: 2

Ingredients:

- 2 lb. of your choice of meat (beef, pork)
- 2 tablespoons soy sauce
- 1 tablespoon vegetable oil
- 1 tablespoon of grated ginger
- 2 cloves of minced garlic

Instructions:

1. Cut your choice of meat into thin strips.
2. In a small bowl, mix grated ginger, soy sauce, vegetable oil, and minced garlic together.
3. Place a wok over high heat and let it heat.
4. Once hot, add the meat and the sauce mixture.
5. Stir-fry for 5-7 minutes or until the meat is cooked through.
6. Serve over rice or noodles.

Nutritional information per serving:

Calories: 431 Proteins: 23 g Fats: 16 g, Carbs: 27

76. Asian Pork Linguine

This dish is perfect for a quick and easy weeknight dinner. The thin strips of pork are cooked to tender perfection in a flavorful soy and brown sugar sauce. The linguine adds a nice texture and is the perfect vehicle for the sauce. You, also, can add vegetables like bell peppers, broccoli, or mushrooms to make it a complete meal.

Prep Time: 15 minutes
Cook Time: 8 minutes
Servings: 5

Ingredients:

- 1 pound pork tenderloin, sliced into thin strips
- ½ cup soy sauce
- 2 cloves garlic, minced
- 2 tablespoons brown sugar
- 8 ounces linguine

Instructions:

1. Prepare the linguine as per the package instructions until al dente. Drain and set aside.
2. In a wok or large skillet, heat a small amount of oil over high heat. Add the sliced pork and stir-fry for 3-4 minutes, until browned.
3. Add the minced garlic and stir-fry for an additional minute.
4. Mix the brown sugar and soy sauce together in a small bowl. Pour the mixture over the pork and stir to coat. Cook for 2-3 more minutes, until the pork is well-cooked and the sauce is thick.
5. Toss the cooked linguine with the pork and sauce. Serve hot, garnished with chopped green onions or cilantro if desired.

Nutritional information per serving:

Calories: 376 Carbs: 39g Fats: 14g, Proteins: 27g

77. Celery with Beef Liver Stir Fry

Celery with Beef Liver Stir Fry is a recipe worth trying if you want to break out of the routine of eating the same dishes over and over again. As an added bonus this dish is healthy, low calorie, and filling!

Prep Time: 10 minutes
Cook Time: 15 minutes
Servings: 4

Ingredients:

- 1 pound beef liver, sliced
- 2 cups sliced celery
- 2 tablespoons oyster sauce
- 2 tablespoons soy sauce
- 2 cloves of garlic, minced

Instructions:

1. In a small bowl, mix the minced garlic soy sauce, and oyster sauce together.
2. Heat a wok over high heat and add the beef liver. Cook for 2-3 minutes, or until the liver is browned and cooked through.
3. Remove the liver from the wok and set aside.
4. In the same wok, add the sliced celery and cook until the celery is slightly softened, or for about 3 minutes.
5. Add the oyster sauce mixture to the wok and stir to combine.
6. Return the cooked beef liver to the wok and toss to coat in the sauce.
7. Cook for 2-3 more minutes, or until the liver is heated through.
8. Serve the beef liver stir fry over rice or noodles and enjoy!

Nutritional information per serving:

Calories: 153 Fats: 7g Carbs: 3g, Proteins: 20g

Note: You can add some vegetables like bell peppers or carrots for more nutritional value and taste. Also, you can use chicken liver instead of beef liver.

78. Ginger and Sesame Pineapple Pork

This recipe is a flavorful and easy dish that combines sweet and savory flavors and is a great Proteins-packed dinner. The ginger and sesame in this recipe are really fragrant and they make the pork really flavorful. Ginger also has excellent anti-inflammatory properties, so your body will be able to heal at a faster rate because of it.

Prep Time: 10 minutes
Cook Time: 15 minutes
Servings: 4

Ingredients:

- 1 oz. pork tenderloin, cut into thin strips
- 1 cup diced pineapple
- 2 tablespoons sesame oil
- 2 tablespoons soy sauce
- 2 tablespoons grated ginger

Instructions:

1. In a small bowl, mix together the sesame oil, soy sauce, and grated ginger.
2. Place a wok over high heat and let it heat and add the pork strips. Cook for 5-7 minutes, or until the pork is browned.
3. Remove pork from the wok and place aside.
4. In the same wok, add the diced pineapple and cook for about 3 minutes, or until the pineapple starts to soften.
5. Add the sesame oil mixture to the wok and stir to combine.
6. Return the cooked pork to the wok and toss to coat in the sauce.
7. Cook 2-3 more minutes, or until the pork is heated through.
8. Serve the pineapple pork over rice or noodles and enjoy!

Nutritional information per serving:

Calories: 228, Fats: 12g, Carbs: 7g, Proteins: 24g

Note: You can add some vegetables like bell peppers or snow peas for more nutritional value and taste.

79. Pepper Meat

Pepper Meat is a delicious and easy to make dish that is perfect for a quick weekend dinner. It's a flavorful blend of tender meat, peppers, and spices that are stir-fried to perfection in a wok.

Prep Time: 10 minutes
Cook Time: 9 minutes
Servings: 3

Ingredients:

- 2 lb. beef or pork, sliced thinly
- 1 red bell pepper, sliced
- 1 green bell pepper, sliced
- 2 cloves of garlic, minced
- 2 tablespoons soy sauce

Instructions:

1. Place a wok over high heat and let it heat. Add a small amount of oil to the pan.
2. Add the sliced meat and cook for 2-3 minutes, or until browned.
3. Remove meat from the pan and place aside.
4. In the same pan, add the sliced bell peppers and minced garlic. Stir-fry for 2-3 minutes, or until the peppers are slightly softened.
5. Put back the browned meat to the pan along with the soy sauce. Stir-fry 2-3 more minutes, or until the meat is cooked through and the sauce is evenly distributed.
6. Serve the pepper meat over rice or noodles.

Nutritional information per serving:

Calories: 250 Fats: 13g Carbs: 7g Proteins: 25g

80. Garlic with Braised Duck Legs

What's better than garlic? Garlic with braised duck legs, of course! If you're looking to create an impressive dish without too much effort, braised duck legs will provide you with all the satisfaction your taste buds desire.

Prep Time: 10 minutes
Cook Time: 44 minutes
Servings: 4

Ingredients:

- 4 duck legs
- 6 cloves of garlic, minced
- ¼ cup soy sauce
- ¼ cup honey
- ¼ cup rice vinegar

Instructions:

1. In a small bowl, mix the honey, soy sauce, and rice vinegar together.
2. Place a wok over high heat and let it heat and add the duck legs, skin-side down. Cook for 5-7 minutes, or until the skin is crispy and browned.
3. Remove the duck legs from the wok and set aside.
4. In the same wok, add the minced garlic and cook for 1-2 minutes, or until fragrant.
5. Add the soy sauce mixture to the wok and stir to combine.
6. Return the duck legs to the wok, skin-side up, and spoon the sauce over the legs.
7. Cover the wok and reduce the heat to low. Cook for 30-35 minutes, or until the duck legs are tender and cooked through.
8. Serve the braised duck legs with the garlic and sauce spooned over the top. Enjoy!

Note: You can add some vegetables like bok choy or broccoli for more nutritional value and taste.

Nutritional information per serving:

Calories: 531, Fats: 33g, Carbs: 24g, Proteins: 34g

81. Sesame Beef

This recipe is a classic Chinese dish that packs a flavorful punch with minimal ingredients. The tender meat and crisp bell peppers are stir-fried with garlic and soy sauce to create a savory, satisfying dish that is perfect for a quick lunch or dinner. It's a great recipe for those who are looking for a simple, yet delicious meal that can be made in under 20 minutes.

Prep Time: 10 minutes
Cook Time: 9 minutes
Servings: 4

Ingredients:

- 3 lb. beef or pork, sliced thinly
- 1 red bell pepper, sliced
- 1 green bell pepper, sliced
- 2 cloves of garlic, minced

- 2 tablespoons soy sauce

Instructions:

1. Place a wok over high heat and let it heat. Add a small amount of oil to the pan.
2. Add the sliced meat and cook for 2-3 minutes, or until browned.
3. Remove the meat from the pan and place aside.
4. In the same pan, add the sliced bell peppers and minced garlic. Stir-fry for 2-3 minutes, or until the peppers are slightly softened.
5. Put back the meat to the pan along with the soy sauce. Stir-fry for 2-3 more minutes, or until the meat is cooked through and the sauce is evenly distributed.
6. Serve the pepper meat over rice or noodles.

Nutritional information per serving:

Calories: 250 Fats: 13g Carbs: 7g Proteins: 25g

82. Asparagus with Steak Stir-Fry

Tired of the same old steamed, boiled, or sautéed asparagus side dish? Get creative with this flavorful steak stir-fry! This dish is a perfect balance of flavors and textures, and it's a great way to elevate a lunch or dinner.

Prep Time: 10 minutes
Cook Time: 15 minutes
Servings: 4

Ingredients:

- 1 pound sirloin steak, sliced thin
- 2 cups asparagus, trimmed
- 2 tablespoons hoisin sauce
- 2 tablespoons rice vinegar
- 2 cloves of garlic, minced

Instructions:

1. In a small bowl, mix the rice vinegar, hoisin sauce, and minced garlic together.
2. Place a wok over high heat and let it heat and add the sirloin steak. Cook for 2-3 minutes, or until the steak is browned and cooked through.
3. Remove the steak from the wok and set aside.
4. In the same wok, add the asparagus and cook for 2-3 minutes, or until the asparagus is slightly softened.
5. Add the hoisin sauce mixture to the wok and stir to combine.
6. Return the cooked steak to the wok and toss to coat in the sauce.
7. Cook for 2-3 more minutes, or until the steak is heated through.
8. Serve the steak stir fry over rice or noodles and enjoy!

Nutritional information per serving:

Calories: 217, Fats: 9g, Carbs: 5g, Proteins: 27g

Note: You can add some vegetables like bell peppers or mushrooms for more nutritional value and taste.

83. Peppered Pork Meatballs

Do you love pork, but are looking for a new twist? These peppered pork meatballs are the perfect recipe for any night of the week. A family favorite, these meatballs will delight both your taste buds and your loved ones! They taste great and if you are a fan of pork, you will definitely love these meatballs. Add them to your shopping list now before it's too late!

Prep Time: 15 minutes
Cook Time: 20 minutes
Servings: 4

Ingredients:

- 1 pound ground pork
- ¼ cup breadcrumbs
- 1 egg
- 2 tablespoons black pepper

- 2 tablespoons olive oil

Instructions:

1. In a large bowl, mix the breadcrumbs, ground pork, egg, and black pepper together until well combined.
2. Roll the mixture into small meatballs, about 1 inch in diameter.
3. Place a wok over high heat and let it heat and add the olive oil.
4. Add the meatballs to the wok and cook for about 10 minutes, or until browned and cooked through, turning occasionally.
5. Serve the pork meatballs with your favorite sauce and enjoy!

Nutritional information per serving:

Calories: 348 Fats: 27g Carbs: 5g Proteins: 21g

Note: You can add some vegetables like bell peppers or mushrooms for more nutritional value and taste.

Chapter 7:

Quick Recipes

84. Coconut Prawns on Lime Noodles

This dish is a delicious combination of sweet and tangy flavors. The red curry paste and fish sauce give it a nice spicy kick, while the coconut milk and lime juice add a touch of sweetness and acidity. The prawns are succulent and tender, and the lime noodles are the perfect complement to the dish. This recipe is perfect for any special occasion.

Prep Time: 10 minutes
Cook Time: 4 minutes
Servings: 3

Ingredients:

- 1 lb. large prawns, peeled and deveined
- 1 can of coconut milk
- 1 tbsp. fish sauce
- ¼ cup lime juice
- 8 oz. rice noodles

Instructions:

1. Prepare the rice noodles as per package instructions, then set aside.
2. In a wok or large pan, heat the coconut milk over medium-high heat.
3. Add fish sauce, stir well.
4. Add prawns and sauté until they turn pink and are cooked through or, for about 3-4 minutes.
5. Remove from heat and add lime juice.
6. Toss the cooked rice noodles with the prawns and sauce.
7. Serve hot.

Nutritional information per serving:

Calories: 119 Carbs: 5g Fats: 3g Proteins: 23g

85. Sausage and Cabbage Wok

This wok dish is savory, with a nice balance of flavors from the soy sauce and oyster sauce. The sesame oil gives the dish a nutty aroma and the sausages provide a nice texture and protein to the dish. The cabbage adds a nice crunch and is a great way to get some greens in your meal. This dish is easy to make, and it's perfect for a quick and hearty weeknight dinner.

Prep Time: 10 minutes
Cook Time: 8 minutes
Servings: 3

Ingredients:

- 1 lb. of sausage (your choice of variety)
- 1 head of green cabbage, thinly sliced
- 1 tbsp. soy sauce
- 1 tbsp. oyster sauce

- 1 tbsp. sesame oil

Instructions:

1. Cut the sausages into bite-size slices.
2. In a wok or large pan, heat the sesame oil over medium-high heat.
3. Add the sausages and stir fry for 2-3 minutes or until they are browned.
4. Add the sliced cabbage and stir fry for another 2-3 minutes or until the cabbage is slightly wilted.
5. Add in the oyster sauce and soy sauce.
6. Cook for another 1-2 minutes or until the sauce is evenly distributed and the cabbage is cooked to your preference.
7. Serve hot.

Nutritional information per serving:

Calories: 431 Carbs: 30g Fats: 16g Proteins: 21g

86. Bok Choy Stir-Fry

Bok Choy Wok Stir-Fry is perfect for a quick dinner any day of the week. The bok choy stir-fry is a simple, yet very flavorful dish. It uses a number of ingredients that work well together in order to create a unique, refreshing taste. This recipe has the potential to go really well with many different types of proteins, giving it versatility and versatility. Bok choy is one type of vegetable that was created because they are so adaptable to almost any situation! or an all-inclusive meal when hosting company. Serve up a family favorite or whip it up as an appetizer dish at your next gathering.

Prep Time: 10 minutes
Cook Time: 8 minutes
Servings: 5

Ingredients:

- 1 pound Bok Choy, cleaned and sliced
- 2 cloves garlic, minced
- 2 tablespoons soy sauce
- 2 tablespoons vegetable oil
- 2 tablespoons sesame oil (optional)

Instructions:

1. Place a wok over high heat and let it heat.
2. Add the vegetable oil and once hot, add the garlic, stir-fry for 1-2 minutes or until fragrant.
3. Add the Bok Choy and stir-fry for 3-5 minutes, or until they are wilted.
4. Add in the soy sauce and sesame oil, and stir-cook for an additional 1-2 minutes.
5. Serve immediately.

Nutritional information per serving:

Calories: 70 Fats: 5g Carbs: 5g Proteins: 2g

87. Amaranth with Vegetables

Amaranth is a nutritious grain that is gluten-free, high in protein and minerals. This dish is a delicious and simple way to enjoy amaranth with mixed vegetables. The soy sauce and sesame oil provide a nice balance of flavors, while the garlic gives it a nice aroma. The mixed vegetables are a great source of vitamins and minerals and the amaranth is a great source of protein. This dish is easy to make and very tasty.

Prep Time: 10 minutes
Cook Time: 29 minutes
Servings: 4

Ingredients:

- 1 cup Amaranth seeds
- 2 cups mixed vegetables (such as carrots, bell peppers, onions, and broccoli)

- 2 cloves garlic, minced
- 1 tbsp. soy sauce
- 1 tbsp. sesame oil

Instructions:

1. Rinse and drain the amaranth seeds.
2. In a pot or saucepan, bring 3 cups of water to a boil.
3. Add the amaranth and reduce the heat to low, cover and simmer for about 20 minutes or until the water is absorbed and the seeds are tender.
4. In a wok or large pan, heat the sesame oil over medium-high heat.
5. Add garlic and stir fry for 1-2 minutes or until fragrant.
6. Add the mixed vegetables and stir fry for 2-3 minutes or until they are slightly wilted.
7. Add soy sauce and stir fry for another 1-2 minutes or until the sauce is evenly distributed and the vegetables are cooked to your preference.
8. Add the cooked amaranth to the pan and stir fry for another 1-2 minutes or until everything is well mixed.
9. Serve hot.

Nutritional information per serving:

Calories: 119 Carbs: 5g Fats: 3g Proteins: 23g

88. Spinach with Crispy Noodles

This dish is a simple and delicious way to enjoy spinach and crispy noodles. The soy sauce and oyster sauce provide a nice balance of flavors, while the garlic gives it a nice aroma. The spinach is a great source of vitamins, and the crispy noodles add a nice crunch to the dish. This dish is easy to make, and it's perfect for a quick and healthy weeknight dinner.

Prep Time: 10 minutes
Cook Time: 7 minutes
Servings: 2

Ingredients:

- 8 oz. of crispy chow mein noodles
- 1 lb. spinach
- 1 tbsp. soy sauce
- 1 tbsp. oyster sauce

- 2 cloves of garlic, minced

Instructions:

1. In a wok or large pan, heat 1 tbsp. of oil over medium-high heat.
2. Add garlic and stir fry for 1-2 minutes or until fragrant.
3. Add spinach and stir fry for 2-3 minutes or until it is wilted.
4. Add soy sauce and oyster sauce, stir well.
5. Add the crispy chow mein noodles and stir fry for 1-2 minutes or until the noodles are heated through and the sauce is evenly distributed.
6. Serve hot.

Nutritional information per serving:

Calories: 261 Carbs: 54g Fats: 1g Proteins: 8g

89. Butternut Squash and Bean Salad

This salad is a perfect combination of flavors and textures. The butternut squash is roasted to bring out its natural sweetness and the cumin powder adds a nice smoky flavor. The black beans are a good source of protein and fiber, while the cilantro and lime add a freshness to the salad. This dish is easy to make, and it's perfect as a side dish or as a main course if you add a protein like grilled chicken or shrimp.

Prep Time: 15 minutes
Cook Time: 20 minutes
Servings: 4

Ingredients:

- 1 lb. butternut squash, peeled and diced
- 1 (4 oz) can black beans, drained and rinsed

- ¼ cup cilantro, chopped
- 1 lime, juiced
- 1 tbsp. oil

Instructions:

1. Preheat the oven to 375°F.
2. On a baking sheet, toss the diced butternut squash with 1 tbsp. of oil, cumin powder and salt.
3. Roast the butternut squash for about 20 minutes or until it is tender.
4. combine the black beans, cilantro, lime juice, and salt to taste in a large bowl,.
5. Add the roasted butternut squash and toss everything together.
6. Serve chilled or at room temperature.

Nutritional information per serving:

Calories: 443 Carbs: 39g Fats: 20g Proteins: 22g

90. Spiced Cashews with Fried Rice

If you like spicy nut mix and flavorful, crunchy rice, then you will love this dish. It is an unusual meal that can entice anyone to try your cooking style. These spices will work their magic on your taste buds and make you want to eat more.

Prep Time: 10 minutes
Cook Time: 7 minutes
Servings: 3

Ingredients:

- 1 cup of raw cashews
- 1 tbsp. vegetable oil
- 1 tsp. cumin powder
- ½ tsp. salt
- 2 cups cooked white rice

Instructions:

1. In a wok or large pan, heat the oil over medium-high heat.
2. Add the cashews and stir fry for 2-3 minutes or until they are lightly toasted.
3. Add cumin powder and salt, stir well.
4. Cook for 1-2 minutes or until the spices are fragrant.
5. Add the cooked rice and stir fry for another 2-3 minutes or until the rice is heated through and the cashews are well mixed in.
6. Serve hot.

Nutritional information per serving:

Calories: 429 Carbs: 45g Fats: 12g Proteins: 12g

91. Wok Scrambled Snow Peas

Are you looking to add some flavor to your day? This crispy snow pea dish will hit it out of the park! It's full of flavor and works well for appetizers, lunchtime salads, or as part of a main meal.

Prep Time: 6 minutes
Cook Time: 5 minutes
Servings: 3

Ingredients:

- 1 pound snow peas, trimmed
- 3 cloves garlic, minced
- 2 tablespoons soy sauce
- 2 tablespoons vegetable oil
- 2 eggs, beaten

Instructions:

1. Place a wok over high heat and let it heat.
2. Add in the vegetable oil and once hot, add the garlic and snow peas, stir-fry for 2-3 minutes or until they are tender-crisp.
3. Push the snow peas to one side of the wok, and add the beaten eggs to the other side. Scramble the eggs quickly, stirring constantly, until they are fully cooked.
4. Mix the eggs with the snow peas and stir in the soy sauce. Cook for an additional 1-2 minutes.
5. Serve immediately.

Nutritional information per serving:

Calories: 120 Fats: 8g Carbs: 8g Proteins: 6g

92. Cauliflower Curry

Cauliflower is a vegetable that you might not have any idea how to cook. They are actually pretty versatile and can be used in different types of dishes. Wok Cauliflower Curry is one of those recipes that would be great for anyone. It cooks cauliflower with curry powder so it becomes super tasty and delicious!

Prep Time: 10 minutes
Cook Time: 20 minutes
Servings: 4

Ingredients:

- 1 head cauliflower, cut into florets
- 2 cloves garlic, minced
- 1 cup curry sauce
- 2 tablespoons vegetable oil
- 2 tablespoons chopped cilantro (optional)

Instructions:

1. Place a wok over high heat and let it heat.
2. Add the vegetable oil and once hot, add the garlic, stir-fry for 1-2 minutes or until fragrant.
3. Add the cauliflower florets and stir-fry for 8-10 minutes or until they are tender.
4. Add the curry sauce, bring it to a boil, lower heat to low, cover and let it simmer for 8-10 minutes or until the cauliflower is cooked through.
5. Stir in the cilantro and cook for an additional 1-2 minutes.
6. Serve immediately.

Nutritional information per serving:

Calories: 150 Fats: 8g Carbs: 14g Proteins: 3g

93. Rump Steak with Stir-Fried Vegetables

This dish is a delicious and simple way to enjoy rump steak with mixed vegetables. The soy sauce and oyster sauce provide a nice balance of flavors, while the garlic gives it a nice aroma. The vegetables are a great source of vitamins and minerals, and the steak is a great source of protein. This dish is easy to make, and it's perfect for a quick and hearty weeknight meal.

Prep Time: 8 minutes
Cook Time: 10 minutes
Servings: 2

Ingredients:

- 1 lb. of rump steak, thinly sliced
- 2 cups of mixed vegetables (such as bell peppers, onions, carrots, and broccoli)
- 2 cloves of garlic, minced

- 1 tbsp. soy sauce
- 1 tbsp. oyster sauce

Instructions:

1. In a wok or large pan, heat 1 tbsp. of oil over medium-high heat.
2. Add garlic and stir fry for 1-2 minutes or until fragrant.
3. Add the sliced steak and stir fry for 2-3 minutes or until it is browned and cooked to your preference.
4. Remove steak from the pan and placee aside.
5. In the same pan, add mixed vegetables and stir fry for 2-3 minutes or until they are slightly wilted.
6. Add soy sauce and oyster sauce, stir well.
7. Add the cooked steak back to the pan and stir fry for another 1-2 minutes or until the sauce is evenly distributed and the vegetables are cooked to your preference.
8. Serve hot.

Nutritional information per serving:

Calories: 315 Carbs: 5g Fats: 10g Proteins: 35g

94. Tempeh with Mango and Shallots

Tempeh is a healthy soybean product that's been fermented and a little bit of fat has been added. It tastes great, it cooks up like meat, and it does not have gluten. The sweet, rich flavor of ripe mango pairs beautifully with the slightly spicy and salty tempeh.

Prep Time: 10 minutes
Cook Time: 9 minutes
Servings: 2

Ingredients:

- 1 lb. tempeh, sliced
- 1 ripe mango, peeled and diced
- 2 shallots, thinly sliced
- 1 tbsp. soy sauce
- 1 tbsp. oil

Instructions:

1. In a wok or large pan, heat 1 tbsp. of oil over medium-high heat.
2. Add the sliced tempeh and stir fry for 2-3 minutes or until it is slightly browned.
3. Add the shallots and stir fry for another 1-2 minutes or until they are softened.
4. Add the diced mango and stir fry for 1-2 minutes or until it is heated through.
5. Add soy sauce, stir well.
6. Cook for another 1-2 minutes or until the sauce is evenly distributed and the tempeh and vegetables are cooked to your preference.
7. Serve hot.

Nutritional information per serving:

Calories: 261| Carbs: 54g| Fats: 1g| Proteins: 8g

95. Wok Garlic Almond Bean Stir-Fry

A scrumptiously flavored stir-fry that will fill your home with an intoxicating scent. Full of incredible flavor, this dish is easy and quick to prepare, perfect for a weeknight meal. With minimal ingredients that you can purchase at any grocery store, this recipe is one of the most accessible stir-fries out there!

Prep Time: 10 minutes
Cook Time: 9 minutes
Servings: 3

Ingredients:

- 1 pound green beans, trimmed
- ½ cup almonds, chopped
- 3 cloves garlic, minced
- 2 tablespoons soy sauce
- 2 tablespoons vegetable oil

Instructions:

1. Place a wok over high heat and let it heat.
2. Add vegetable oil and heat add the garlic and almonds, stir-fry for 1-2 minutes or until fragrant.
3. Add the green beans and stir-fry for 3-5 minutes, or until they are tender-crisp.
4. Add in the soy sauce, and stir-cook for an additional 1-2 minutes.
5. Serve immediately.

Nutritional information per serving:

Calories: 200 Fats: 17g Carbs: 10g Proteins: 6g

96. Spicy Red Pepper and Cucumber

This simple stir-fry is a great way to enjoy red bell pepper and cucumber in a new and delicious way. The chili sauce adds a nice kick of heat to this dish. The garlic adds a good depth of flavor. This recipe is a healthy and easy to make side dish.

Prep Time: 5 minutes
Cook Time: 7 minutes
Servings: 2

Ingredients:

- 1 red bell pepper, sliced
- 1 cucumber, sliced

- 2 cloves garlic, minced
- 2 tablespoons chili sauce
- 2 tablespoons vegetable oil

Instructions:

1. Place a wok over high heat and let it heat.
2. Add the oil and heat it. Add the garlic and red bell pepper, stir-fry for about 3 minutes or until they are tender-crisp.
3. Add the cucumber and stir-fry for 1-2 minutes more.
4. Stir in the chili sauce, and cook for an additional 1-2 minutes.
5. Serve immediately.

Nutritional information per serving:

Calories: 80 Fats: 7g Carbs: 5g Proteins: 1g

97. Sichuan Eggplant in Sauce

An unusual dish from Sichuan, China, and this mouth-watering recipe is one of those dishes you can't help but keep coming back to. The curry-like sauce provides a unique harmony to the soft eggplant.

Prep Time: 10 minutes
Cook Time: 9 minutes
Servings: 2

Ingredients:

- 1 pound eggplant, sliced
- 2 cloves garlic, minced
- 2 tablespoons Sichuan sauce (or any spicy Chinese sauce)
- 2 tablespoons vegetable oil
- 2 tablespoons scallions, chopped

Instructions:

1. Place a wok over high heat and let it heat.
2. Add the oil and heat. Add the garlic and eggplant, stir-fry for 3-5 minutes or until they are tender-crisp.
3. Stir in the Sichuan sauce, and cook for an additional 1-2 minutes.
4. Add the scallions and stir-fry for 1-2 minutes more.
5. Serve immediately.

Nutritional information per serving:

Calories: 13 Fats: 10g Carbs: 9g Proteins: 2g

98. Scrambled Potato and Green Beans

Bored of your same old grub? Take a break from it with this scrumptious recipe. These spiced-up mashed potatoes and green beans will be the perfect breakfast for health-conscious cooks and children alike, this dish is easy to make and delicious. The green beans also provide a healthy dose of vitamins and antioxidants to protect you from an unhealthy range of daily environmental toxins that can be harmful to your body.

Prep Time: 10 minutes
Cook Time: 14 minutes
Servings: 3

Ingredients:

- 1 pound potatoes, peeled and diced
- 1 pound green beans, trimmed
- 2 cloves garlic, minced

- 2 tablespoons vegetable oil
- 2 eggs, beaten

Instructions:

1. Place a wok over high heat and let it heat.
2. Add the oil and heat. Add the garlic and potatoes, stir-fry for 5-7 minutes or until they are tender.
3. Add the green beans and stir-fry for 3-5 minutes or until they are tender-crisp.
4. Push the potato and green beans to one side of the wok, and add the beaten eggs to the other side. Scramble the eggs quickly, stirring constantly, until they are fully cooked.
5. Mix the eggs with the potatoes and green beans. Cook for an additional 1-2 minutes.
6. Serve immediately.

Nutritional information per serving:

Calories: 250 Fats: 12g Carbs: 30g Proteins: 8g

99. Bacon-Wrapped Hot Dogs

Bacon-wrapped hot dogs are an excellent addition to any event. They're easy to make, and will have everyone begging for more. This wok-made recipe will have you enjoying crispy, salty bacon wrapped hot dogs in no time.

Prep Time: 15 minutes
Cook Time: 14 minutes
Servings: 8

Ingredients:

- 8 hot dogs
- 8 slices bacon, cut in half
- 2 cloves garlic, minced
- 2 tablespoons Worcestershire sauce
- 2 tablespoons vegetable oil

Instructions:

1. Place a wok over high heat and let it heat.
2. Wrap bacon slices around the hot dogs.
3. Add the vegetable oil and once hot, add the garlic, stir-fry for 1-2 minutes or until fragrant.
4. Add the bacon-wrapped hot dogs to the wok and stir-fry for 8-10 minutes or until the bacon is crispy and the hot dogs are heated through.
5. Stir in the Worcestershire sauce and cook for an additional 1-2 minutes.
6. Serve immediately.

Nutritional information per serving:

Calories: 300 Fats: 26g Carbs: 2g Proteins: 12g

100. Crispy French Fries

At the end of a long, tough day, we all need some comfort. Some really good food to take the edge off. And if this is you, then I know for sure that French fries are your go-to. This recipe is for a new take on crispy, crunchy fries that are wok-made and deep fried. These fries are amazing and you will love them!

Prep Time: 10 minutes
Cook Time: 5 minutes
Servings: 2

Ingredients:

- 1 lb. russet potatoes, peeled and sliced into fries
- 2 cups vegetable oil

- 1 tsp. salt
- 1 tsp. garlic powder
- 1 tsp. paprika

Instructions:

1. Place a wok over high heat and let it heat. Add vegetable oil.
2. Rinse the potato slices and dry them with a paper towel.
3. Add the potatoes to the wok in small batches and cook for about 5 minutes, or until golden brown and crispy.
4. Use a slotted spoon to remove the French fries and place them on a plate lined with paper towel to drain off excess oil.
5. Sprinkle salt, garlic powder, and paprika over the fries and toss to coat.
6. Serve immediately while still hot and crispy.

Nutritional information per serving:

Calories: 548 Proteins: 4g Fats: 38g Carbs: 57g

Conclusion

Thank you for reaching the end of this book. This 5-Ingredients Wok Cookbook for Beginners has been designed to provide a comprehensive guide for those new to wok cooking. With 100 easy-to-follow recipes, you will find a variety of dishes to suit every taste, from traditional Chinese recipes to modern twists on classic dishes.

I can literally feel your enthusiasm for preparing food with the wok. Contrary to what many people believe beforehand, working with this special pan offers much more potential than you thought at the beginning. But you will also notice that the theoretical part in this book is actually necessary at the start in order to be able to integrate the best equipment and pragmatic hand movements into this culinary bonfire. Whether as a tasteful entertainment at the table, for a small bite for in between or nevertheless in the context of an opulently created and impressive (family) dinner - the wok always serves you well and gives you some wonderful plus points when cooking at home. If you take the tips for using the pan, which originated in China, to heart, you will not only treat yourself and your loved ones to delicious meals, but also to the particularly intense taste sensation of high-quality oils, herbs, vegetables and many other natural products. Thanks to the short cooking time, the wok is also fantastically time-efficient, because if there's one thing you don't have on hand, it's time! But the quickly prepared wok dishes allow for a healthy and varied diet every day, at lunchtime or in the evening, as well as alone or with the entire household. But not at the end of the positive aspects, the wok also offers you and your loved ones a rich nutritional supply without wasting ingredients.

The five ingredients used in each recipe have been carefully chosen to provide a balance of flavors, textures, and nutrients. The use of fresh, healthy ingredients ensures that your meals are not only delicious but also good for you. The wok can be used to create a wide range of dishes, from stir-fries to soups, and the recipes in this cookbook are a great starting point for experimenting with new flavors and techniques.

The cookbook is divided into chapters that cover different types of dishes, such as rice recipes, fish and seafood recipes, chicken and poultry recipes, noodles recipes, beef, pork, and lamb recipes, and quick recipes. Each recipe includes clear, step-by-step instructions, making it easy for beginners to follow. The book also includes helpful tips and tricks for wok cooking, such as how to properly season your wok, how to stir-fry, and how to create the perfect sauce.

One of the key advantages of this cookbook is that it is designed to be easy to follow, even for those who have never cooked with a wok before. The recipes are simple, yet delicious, and are perfect for busy individuals who want to cook healthy and tasty meals at home. The ingredients used in the recipes are easy to find at any local grocery store and are not expensive, making it accessible for everyone.

In addition, the cookbook also includes a list of essential wok cooking tools and equipment. This is a great resource for those who are new to wok cooking and are not sure what they need to get started. The cookbook also includes a section on how to properly care for your wok, so that it will last for a long time.

Overall, this 5-Ingredients Wok Cookbook for Beginners is an excellent resource for anyone interested in learning how to cook with a wok. The recipes are easy to follow, the ingredients are readily available, and the results are delicious. Whether a beginner or an experienced cook, this cookbook has something to offer. With the help of this cookbook, you will be able to create delicious, healthy meals that are sure to impress your friends and family.

Exclusive 5-day bonus course just for you!

We will be sharing more cooking techniques, tips and delicious recipes that will elevate your cooking to the next level!

Simply let us know where to send the course e-mails to via this link below.

https://bit.ly/michelle-tan-bgp

For any general feedback & enquiries, you can reach us at bookgrowthpublishing@mail.com

Measurement Conversions

Volume Equivalents (Liquid)

Us Standard	Us standard (ounces)	Metric (approximate)
2 tablespoons	1 fl. oz.	30 mL
¼ cup	2 fl. oz.	60 mL
½ cup	4 fl. oz.	120 mL
1 cup	8 fl. oz.	240 mL
1½ cups	12 fl. oz.	355 mL
2 cups or 1 pint	16 fl. oz.	475 mL
4 cups or 1 quart	32 fl. oz.	1 L
1 gallon	128 fl. oz.	4 L

Volume Equivalents (Dry)

US Standard	Metric (approximate)
⅛ teaspoon	0.5 mL
¼ teaspoon	1 mL
½ teaspoon	2 mL
¾ teaspoon	4 mL
1 teaspoon	5 mL
1 tablespoon	15 mL
¼ cup	59 mL
⅓ cup	79 mL
½ cup	118 mL
⅔ cup	156 mL
¾ cup	177 mL
1 cup	235 mL
2 cups or 1 pint	475 mL
3 cups	700 mL
4 cups or 1 quart	1 L